Around Man[c]

in the 1960s

Not a brush in sight. In October 1964, six members of Salford Corporation Cleansing Department swapped their brushes and shovels for American-built, petrol-driven suction machines. The machines share a family resemblance to *Noo-noo*, the vacuum cleaner in Ragdoll Productions' TV series *Teletubbies*.

Clive Hardy

*i*Nostalgia

iNostalgia is an imprint of Communities in the Cloud Ltd, Progress Centre, Charlton Place, Ardwick, Manchester M12 6HS, UK

ISBN 978-1-84547-243-6

As part of this book, we are delighted to preserve in print some of the wonderful memories we receive every day on our iNostalgia Facebook page. We greatly enjoy reading them and we're sure you will too. If you want to join the conversation, just click on our Facebook page. We'd love to hear from you, www.facebook.com/inostalgiamanchester/

Manchester United fans return home from Wembley following the Red Devils' 4-1 victory over Benfica in the European Cup on 29 May 1969.

Introduction

The idea to compile this book came about during discussions as to whether we should reprint *Around Manchester in the 50s & 60s* which we had published in 2003. It took just a few minutes for us to knock that idea on the head; the main reason being that many of the photographs had appeared in several other publications and quite frankly they'd been done to death. We then decided to split the book in two – *Around Manchester in the 1950s* and *Around Manchester in the 1960s* – allowing us to publish several hundred additional images. There are at least 350 in this volume alone.

The book follows our usual scheme. It is divided into topic-related sections, each of which may or may not have images from Manchester, Salford, Stockport, Bolton, Bury, Oldham, Widnes, Wigan, Rochdale or various points in between all mixed together. The exceptions to this are in the sections *Funny Game Football* and *Grandstand?* Here images relating to Bury FC, Bolton Wanderers, Manchester City, Manchester United, Rochdale FC, Widnes RLFC, Wigan RLFC, Leigh RLFC etc., are in individual subsections.

The first section, *Tin Baths II*, continues from where we left off in *Around Manchester in the 1950s*. Slum clearance continues at a pace around the area. However, even before some developments have been completed, the signs are there that high-rise is not turning out to be the revolution in social housing that planners and architects thought it would be. High-rise was politically expedient – and cheap – but many tower blocks turned out to be a nightmare for their tenants. Once close-knit communities were ripped apart as neighbours, friends and extended families were scattered. The noise you might have got from neighbours either side of you in a row of terraces could now come from either side, as well as below and above – and possibly from people you no longer knew. No one seemed to take responsibility for public space with the result that many landings became litter traps, stairwells and lifts stank of urine. The Corporation Cleansing Department were not going to take on the job, and the very nature of the new blocks put off many tenants from doing it for themselves. People who had lived close to their place of work now found themselves living miles away, though as early as 1965, Rochdale had started to build blocks in the town centre.

That there were problems with some of the new building techniques employed during construction came home to roost during 1969, when a gas explosion in one flat caused an entire corner of the twenty-three storey Ronan Point tower block to collapse.

The next section, *Growing up in the Sixties*, takes a look at school, play, Whit Walks and Christmas. The Sixties was the decade when business woke up to the fact that there was a whole new market out there – the teenager. Clothes, music, books, films, TV (*Top of the Pops*, and *Ready, Steady, Go!*) and radio – "*Radio Caroline on 199!*" It was probably the first decade that teenage girls did not wear clothes like their mothers. Minis, jeans with fly-front zips, PVC jackets and caps defined the generations.

World of Work, looks at coal mining, Trafford Park, Manchester Docks, Beyer, Peacock & Co, textiles, and so on. There are several images of industrial disputes, including that at textile machinery manufacturers Arundel-Coulthard, Chestergate, Stockport. This was a company where there had never been any industrial unrest, that is until it was taken over by the Americans. See page 45 for the full story.

On the Move, looks at transport during the Sixties. New motorways, the increase in car ownership – from 5.6million in 1960 to 11.8million by the end of the decade. In 1965 a Morris Minor Traveller cost £583 and a Rover 2000 cost £1298, though the defining cars of the decade were the Mini and the E-type Jaguar. By the end of the Sixties, 600 miles of motorways were available to thrash them on. We also look at the expansion at Manchester Airport, electrification of the railways and the battle between British Railways and British European Airways for passengers on the lucrative Manchester-London-Manchester routes. The section isn't all smiles as we have included a couple of pages of images taken in the aftermath of the Stockport air disaster and given similar treatment to the train crash at Cheadle Hulme on 28 May 1964.

People and Places looks around the area. There are images taken around Manchester such as the Kardomah in Market Street. It was the decade when going out for a meal took off. Berni Inns, the Forte chain and Pizza Express were launched. In 1965 a Pizza Margherita would have cost you 5/6d (27.5p) and a bottle of red house wine a staggering 14/6d (72.5p). A Wimpy brunch cost 4/9d (24p) and their special grill 5/9d (29p).

The section includes some famous faces of the time. We have Tory leader Ted Heath having a Christmas splurge before heading back to London. We also have Sir Oswald Moseley on the stump at Alexandra Park and Prime Minister, Sir Alec Douglas-Hume, at the Bear Pit, Stockport. Irish MP Bernadette Devlin is pictured at Manchester University and Cosmonaut Yuri Gagarin is seen with Sir Bernard Lovell at Manchester Town Hall. The difficult part comes at the end – *The Moors Murders*.

Grandstand? Looks at athletics, boxing, cricket, tennis, horse racing and rugby league. *Funny Game Football* covers some of the League clubs in the area as well as the then non-league side Wigan Athletic.

In *Rock, Pop, Rhythm & Blues*, we have images including Georgie Fame, the Mudlarks, Eden Kane, the Beatles at Wigan ABC and the ABC Ardwick. Freddie and the Dreamers, Dave Clarke Five, the Rolling Stones, BeeGees, Wayne Fontana and the Mindbenders, the Hollies, Cilla, and the Monkees. That British groups went on to dominate the US music scene is probably due to a girl by the name of Marsha Albert who wrote to disc jockey Carol James and asked him to play the Beatles' *I Want to Hold Your Hand*. It took off and the rest, as they say, is history. Soon, if British bands were not touring the UK, they were away touring the US. The Dave Clarke Five sold one million records a month during their first six months and were the first UK group to undertake a tour of the USA. The Rolling Stones, classed as the bad boys of the British pop invasion, played a mix of blues, R&B and delta blues and along with the Animals and the Yardbirds reintroduced it into mainstream American music.

The last section, *That's Entertainment*, includes a series of images taken on the *Coronation Street* set at Granada.

Just a word of two about prices and costings in the book. They are given in pounds, shillings and pence with the metric equivalent in brackets where necessary. However, you will need to use the inflation calculator to bring them up to 2017 levels. For example, an item costing £1.10s.0d (£1.50p) in 1962 needs to be multiplied by 20.11 to bring it to its 2017 cost of £30.16 – you might need to round up or down. During the 1960s, prices could be written several ways but they all meant the same, so £1.10s.0d (£1.50p) could be written as £1/10/0 or £1/10/- or 30/¬- (thirty shillings), similarly 6s.9d (34p) could be written as 6/9d, or 6/9.

Conversions are: 6d = 2.5p; 1 shilling = 5p; half-a-crown or 2s.6d or 2/6d = 12.5p; 5s.0d or 5/- = 25p; 10s.0d or 10/- = 50p; £1.0s.0d or £1/-/- = 100p. By the late-60s specialist outlets as well as family-run corner shops could trade on Sundays. In some of the advertisements reproduced in the book, some prices are given in guineas. A guinea was 21/- (twenty-one shillings) or £1.1s.0d (£1.5p) and a half guinea was 10s.6d or 10/6 (52.5p). So, three guineas £3.3s.0d (£3.15p) would be written either as 3gns or 3Gns. In 1969 a 3ft wide divan bed could be bought for seven and a half guineas equating to £7.17s.6d (£17.88p). To find its 2017 equivalent multiply £17.88 by 15.66. The inflation calculator for the decade is: 1960 21.01; 1961 20.80; 1962 20.11; 1963 19.28; 1964 18.91; 1965 18.30; 1966 17.46; 1967 16.81; 1968 16.40 and 1969 15.66. Have fun.

As we always state, these books are not academic works nor do we cover everything. So, put the cat out and the kettle on. Sit back, turn the pages and enjoy our look at what was and is *Around Manchester in the 1960s*.

Acknowledgements

This book would not be possible if it were not for the talents of *Manchester Evening News* photographers and journalists Tony Cordt, John Holland, Clive Cooksey, Eric Graham, Bill Batchelor, Mike Grimes, John Featherstone, John Fowler and Ian Currie as well as journalists David Bainton, Ann Sunderland, Barbara Duncan, Chris Stewart, Neal Keeling, Chris Aspen, Beryl Jones, Gerald Brown, Jill Burdett, Peter Gardner, Keith Ward, Janine Watson, John Trickett, Eric Thornton, John Kay, Tom Buist and Brian Hope. Also, we must thank Simon Flavin and John Mead at Mirrorpix for assistance.

Tin Baths part II

Terraced houses in Hulme probably towards the end of 1961. The image was published several times in the *Manchester Evening News*, especially during the 1970s when the city was debating whether it ought to improve rather than demolish unfit housing. By the end of 1967, it was estimated that in England and Wales there were 5million people living in 1.8million slums unfit for human habitation. A further 12million people were thought to be living in homes fit for habitation but lacking one or more basic facilities such as a bathroom, an inside toilet, mains sewerage, or their own water supply.

Number Two Court, Dickinson Street, Oldham, 1 June 1962.

This photograph, taken in Northenden during 1962, depicts a typical communal backyard often associated with slum housing. The scene would have been played out all over the UK, especially in its industrial heartlands. The toilet block is behind the lady pegging out her washing. If you were lucky your family had its own toilet, if unlucky then you shared with one or more other families. If not lagged, the pipes would freeze in winter and it was no joke tramping out to the loo in the freezing rain in the middle of the night. Toilet paper choices were *Izal* – which doubled as tracing paper - or squares of old newspaper hung by a piece of string from a nail. A tin bath hangs on the wall behind the other lady.

On bath night, the tub would be dragged indoors and placed in front of the fire. It was not unusual to take turns. A jug or two of hot water might be added at the change-over, otherwise everyone used the same water. Then came the fun of emptying the damn thing. Kids of today would be horrified at not being able to lock themselves in a cosy, heated bathroom.

A housewife busily 'stoning' her front step. Nelson Street, Manchester, December 1961.

Facebook Memories

Steve Pownall – I was born on Dickinson Street court and appeared in a documentary with my mother Joyce Pownall. My sister and I were filmed when we were very young having a bath in a tin tub. The houses had toilets at the very bottom of the court.

Mark Wheeler – I remember my grandmother's outside loo – and the pipes bursting in the winter when it got really cold! And then there was the *Izal* toilet paper. It really was like grease-proof paper!

Linda Thompson – We used to follow the coal lorry back to its depot in Moss Side, picking up pieces of coal as they fell off and put them in an old child trolley to take home.

Ian Elliott – I remember going with my Mam's wash-house pram for coal bricks and coal nuts from a local coal yard – now the Midway Hotel in Levenshulme.

And now for something completely different'. John Worthington spent the winter months of 1967-68 building this 16ft cabin cruiser on the roof at the back of his terraced house in Salford. Pictured with him are his wife Beryl and their son Robert. Must have been fun getting it down.

Facebook Memories

William Walker – My Dad was a chimney sweep and would ride his bike with his rods ties to the crossbar and sacks of soot on the handle-bars.

John Richardson – Grandad used to tell me about how the whole family shared the bath on bath night. Didn't want to be last!

Jim Etherington – Everyone looked out for each other in the old streets. We all knew each other and knew when folk were ill or needed help.

Spring 1968 and the £4million housing development at Hulme is progressing to schedule. The focal point of the development by architects Hugh Wilson and J Lewis Womersley, was four south-facing crescents, consisting mainly of a mix of two and three bedroom maisonettes. Womersley had designed the award-winning Park Hill flats at Sheffield, a development hailed at the time by architects, planners and sociologists alike as one of the most significant housing schemes for decades.

Yet even as the Hulme redevelopment gathered momentum, trouble was brewing over at Park Hill. Things were not going to plan. Stairwells stank of urine, walkways had become litter traps, vandalism was rife and structural problems were already emerging as steelwork rusted and concrete began to crumble. Within a very short time Park Hill was renamed by its residents – they preferred to call it San Quentin.

Work on the 500-home Coverdale Crescent development began in the late 1960s. As with similar architectural masterpieces of this type, Coverdale Crescent soon acquired a nickname – in this case Fort Ardwick. As a housing project, it was a disaster. Only thirteen years after its completion, a structural survey revealed there had been a considerable amount of water penetration from the flat roofs and access decks and steel fixings were corroding at an alarming rate, causing concrete to crumble.

In less than eight years, Hulme changed beyond all recognition. More than 5000 new homes had been built of which about 60per cent were of the deck-access type. In this image, you can clearly see the four crescents of Hulme 5 – each one named after an architect. Adam, Barry, Nash and Kent. Slums cleared during the years immediately following the war were replaced with a mixture of conventional houses, double-deck maisonettes and walk-up flats. The problems came during the 1960s when councils switched to system-built high-rise blocks and deck-access apartments. These were often poorly designed and the quality of the construction more than questionable. Structural faults abounded. There were problems with sewage disposal and waste collection. Central heating systems packed in more than they worked. There were also serious problems with vermin infestations. Problems with public areas were similar to those already mentioned in the introduction. Stairwells began to stink of urine, walkways became litter traps and vandalism in some blocks was rife.

As with many similar developments of the day, those who wielded power had opted for a quick fix of 'Get things up, get the people in'. Even before it was completed, Hulme was fast becoming a disaster in social engineering. The 1970s would see a return to more traditional types of housing. However, the damage had been done and millions of pounds squandered. The Hulme Study, published in 1990, examined what had happened to bring about the destruction of an entire community. *Evening News* journalist Janine Watson was tasked with studying the report. It left no doubt that what had originally been hailed as a fully planned environment had deteriorated into 'an area of physical dereliction and economic and social distress'.

The community had no focal point. 'Shopping facilities are often in poor locations and they are invariably dirty, dilapidated, unwholesome and intimidating'. Hulme 1 had the oldest but some of the best property of the estate – it also had a stable population. Hulme 2 had deck-access homes plagued with crumbling concrete, the tenants frustrated by the lack of redevelopment. Hulme 3 had 800 deck-access homes in such poor structural condition that demolition was probably the only option. Hulme 4 consisted of the best deck-access homes in Hulme, about 400 in all, but even these required repairs totalling £11million. The crescents of Hulme 5 were already empty and vandalised before the study was launched. The study also identified that much of the population was transient, passing flats informally between themselves, the council and its rules totally ignored. The study also revealed there had been widespread use of asbestos in Hulme's construction – an already acknowledged health risk, 'unpleasant for the occupants and financially disastrous for Manchester city council'. Just to add to the problems, it was found that half the men and 20per cent of women were unemployed. Hulme had deteriorated into one of the worst housing estates in Europe.

By the late 1960s, Salford's Ordsall flats needed refurbishing, but because they were still relatively modern, Whitehall refused to allocate funds. For several years, tenants had put up with steadily deteriorating conditions, which during the winter could prove particularly hard. The flats were fitted with steel window frames and over the years many of these had buckled and parted company from the walls. The resulting gaps – up to an inch wide - let in the howling winter winds. Also, for reasons best known to the architects, the bedrooms were not fitted with power points, forcing older residents to sleep in their living rooms. The size of the kitchen was another cause for complaint. There was no space for modern white goods appliances. The bathroom was where the washing machine went.

Evening News journalist David Bainton described conditions, including overcrowding. 'One of the three-bedroom flats housed a couple and their eight children. The kitchen was too small for a dining table, which along with the food cupboard was in the couple's bedroom. Four girls slept in two single beds in one bedroom. In the other, three boys shared a double bed and the eldest son had a put-u-up'. Things only got worse when Salford switched to North Sea gas. Tenants had their heated drying cabinets disconnected as Salford couldn't afford the cost of converting them. The only way left to dry clothes at home was in front of the living room fire and that tended to fill the flat with condensation.

Langley Middleton was one of 22 overspill estates used by Manchester City Council. The scheme was intended to provide 4000 new dwellings, though the 13-storey blocks shown here were not part of the original plan. Their inclusion added another 700 homes. It is estimated that between 1951-71, more than 200,000 people were rehoused in these estates.

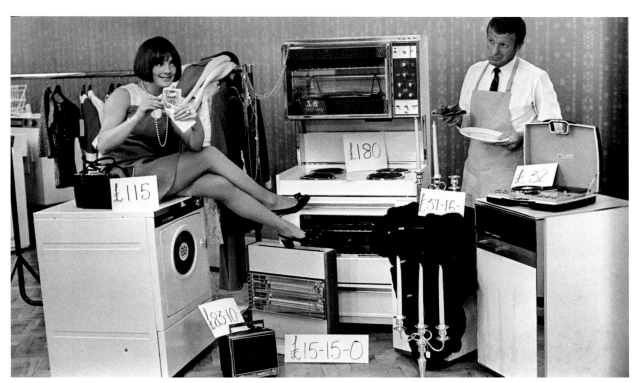

Living the dream in November 1969? All things electric appear to be the order of the day. The 1969 prices for some of these items were: portable telly £83.10s.0d (£83.50p), electric oven £180.0s.0d, portable record player £32.0s.0d, two-bar electric fire £15.15s.0d (£15.75p) and tumble dryer at £115.0s.0d. In some outlets, the price of the two-bar electric fire would have been displayed as 15Gns (fifteen guineas).

(Left) This image was taken on 13 April 1967 and published the following week in the *Manchester Evening News* with the caption: 'Perky little lads, full of energy as they dart along the raised pavement beside tall, gnarled railings. Though present surroundings may be drab and dismal, the future is green and happy. That's the prospect that faces these children in the streets of Ordsall, when their homes are pulled down and they move to new Salford Corporation council estates'.

(Above) Football stars in the making? After all, it is how David Herd and Dennis Viollet started. They kicked a ball around the streets of Moss Side. In 1967 it was still possible to play out in many of the back streets. This is Archie Street, Salford. The church is St Clement's.

(Left) Youngsters look on as Miss Beatrice Tucker goes for the potato puffs. Miss Tucker's corner sweetshop in Thorpe Street, Ordsall, would soon be nothing more than a childhood memory. It is April 1967 and the area is scheduled for demolition.

Growing up in the Sixties

This image was taken in 1960 in what was then known as the Housecraft Section of the newly opened Ordsall Secondary Modern School for Girls and published in the *Manchester Evening News* under 'Housewives of Tomorrow' - so no stereotyping there then. The cookery classroom was equipped with some of the latest labour-saving devices then available.

(Right) Ordsall's Housecraft Section was advanced in that it was set up to replicate a typical modern high-rise flat. The girls were taught how to make beds, lay the table and tidy up. A friend of mine who went to a girls' grammar school remembered her class being taught how to change a mains fuse – it was done by the physics teacher. However, they were not shown how to change a washer on a tap, or where to look to turn the gas or water off in an emergency.

(Below) In January 1964, it was a new term at a new school for the 400 pupils of Broughton High School for Girls. Workmen were still putting the finishing touches to the £300,000 school and a leaking boiler resulted in the girls moving in just two days behind schedule. The old school, about a mile away in Bury New Road, had previously been the home of the Greek consul. It was scheduled for demolition to make way for a new primary school.

Queen Elizabeth II pays a visit to a Manchester school. March 1965.

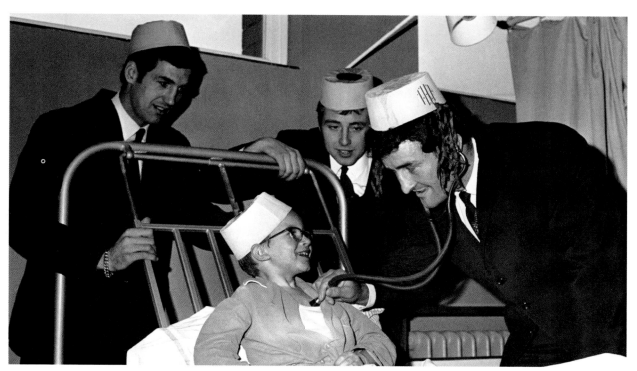

Just what the doctor ordered. Bolton Wanderers players Charlie Hurley, John Hulme and John Byrom pay a visit to the children's ward at Bolton General Hospital during December 1969. 'Doctor' Hurley practises his stethoscope skills on eight-years-old Mark Seddon.

Smiles all round from Charlie Hurley of Bolton Wanderers and five-years-old Anthony Foy, as Charlie puts the ward's bear, Yogi, onto Anthony's bed.

(Above left). 15-year-old Manchester City fan Nigel Shadbolt, was in St Mary's hospital, Paddington, in December 1969, awaiting a kidney transplant, when he was visited by six of his footballing heroes. Prior to playing and defeating West Ham United, Francis Lee, Tony Book, Mike Summerbee, coach Malcolm Allison, Alan Oakes and Mike Doyle turned up with playing kit and photographs for Nigel. (Above right). Manchester United player Bobby Charlton on a visit with the 1963 FA Cup to children in Booth Hall Hospital, where he signed autographs and handed out souvenir programmes.

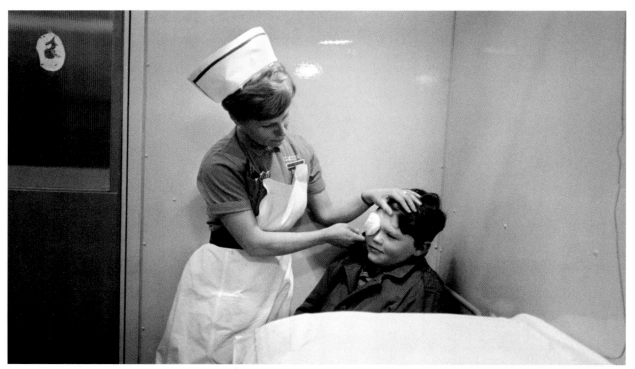

Nurse Elizabeth Scanlon treats a boy for a firework burn. November 1969.

The Hatton triplets from Manchester, Deborah, Sharon and Allison with their baby sister Helen on 3 December 1963. The twins were again photographed on 10 May 1968, by which time they were terrorising their teachers at school.

All the images on this page were taken during the Manchester Whit Walks, June 1960.

The annual Whit Walks began during the early 1800s. Contingents from various local churches, chapels and Sunday schools walked in procession through the streets of Manchester to profess their faith. My mother and her sister each got a new dress every year in time for the annual walk. They were made by my grandmother.

Hot from their Whit Walk and money in their hands, it's decision time as to which ice cream to have. Not that there was a massive choice back in 1960, though that was changing, as Walls had recently doubled their capacity by opening a new factory in Gloucester. The choice tended to be tubs at 4d each (2p), choc ices – at the time they were called chocolate coated ice creams at 3d each (2p), cornets 3d each (2p) and wafers 3d each (2p). The large tubs of ice cream we have today did not exist, however it was possible to buy a block for one shilling.

Wrapped in card, the block was a single flavour, usually vanilla, though sometimes strawberry or chocolate ones were available. For the adventurous amongst you, there was the Neapolitan, a block comprising all three flavours and guaranteed to cause squabbles when it came to sharing it out. *Mister Softee* soft ice cream was still a novelty, having been introduced from America during 1958. The *Mister Softee 99* - soft ice cream in a cone with a Cadbury's flake rammed into the top - was expensive at 6d each (2.5p).

Whit Walkers in Albert Square, Manchester, June 1962.

December 1960. Christmas is coming and the geese are getting fat. Children look longingly at toys in a shop window. It was still a time when Christmas for most children resulted in an annual or two such as *The Beano, The Dandy*, perhaps *Rupert Bear*, a toy or two and a selection box. There were few toys linked to TV or film tie-ins, though I remember in the 1950s having a *Davy Crockett* hat for Christmas following the UK release of the Disney movie *Davy Crockett*. TV tie-ins included a model of Noddy's car by Corgi, Pinky and Perky puppets, and characters from *The Flowerpot Men* and *Andy Pandy*.

If you were very lucky, you might get a toy from the US where children had had TV tie-in stuff since the late-1940s. One Christmas I had a *Johnny Ringo Western Frontier* playset, bought by an uncle who was in the merchant navy. In 1961 Gerry Anderson's *Supercar* took children's programmes into a new dimension with shows that combined science fiction, action, and adventure with puppets. It was quickly followed by *Fireball XL5, Thunderbirds, Stingray* and *Captain Scarlet and the Mysterons*. Naturally toys and annuals followed.

Even adult TV programmes and movies produced spinoffs for children such as Simon Templar's (The Saint) car and James Bond's Aston Martin. The Sixties would bring about a revolution in children's toys.

Blue Peter is the world's longest running children's TV programme and this picture featuring Peter Purves and John Noakes was taken on 8 December 1969, just four days after the launch of the programme's Christmas appeal for unwanted toy metal cars. These were then sold for scrap, the money raised being used to buy four buses and other equipment to provide transport for old people in the UK. The origins of the programme go back to the 16 October 1958, when the *Children's Television Club* was aired for the first time.

The 15-minute programme from the Wallasey Corporation ferry *Royal Iris* featured Judith Chalmers as the presenter and was networked around the UK by BBC Manchester. Though transmitted just once a month, Owen Reed, head of BBC Children's Television, was so impressed with the programme that he negotiated its move to the BBC Television Centre. He was also involved in changing the programme's name to *Blue Peter*.

Batman and Robin escort Father Christmas to Lewis's Store, Market Street, Manchester. The dynamic duo proved just as popular with the kids as Santa. The *Caped Crusader* and the *Boy Wonder* made good their escape.

Santa chats to six-years-old Paula Gould and her brother Philip. Lewis's Store, December 1969.

Simon Dingley, aged four, of Arthur Street, Little Lever, was so upset when he saw on TV that Santa had been arrested that he wrote an appeal to the police. PC George Fobersley from Bolton police paid a visit and a call to the station assured Simon that Santa would be around as usual on Christmas Eve.

(Above left). The most popular toy of the year for 1966 was the Action Man Commando. Here, ten-year-old David Jackson of West Kirby, gets to try out a commando outfit based on the toy. It retailed at 39 shillings (£1.95p) and his toy Browning Automatic Rifle (BAR) at 28/4d (£1.42p). The photograph was taken at the TA Depot, Oldham, in April 1967. With David are Sgt Major Harry Bush and Pvt Bob Thompson of the 1st Battalion Parachute Regiment.

(Above right) Think we can hazard a guess at what this young man had for Christmas 1967 as *High Noon* comes to the wild frontier of Collyhurst.

(Below left). Fun in the snow. Ten-month-old Susan Turkington of Regent Road, Stockport, gets a tow along the snow-clad slopes of Lyme Park, Disley, from her three-year-old sister Linda. 20 January 1960.

(Below right). Growing up in Moss Side in the late 1960s. These children's only nearby playground was heaps of rubble from demolished buildings. Not so different to those of us who grew up during the fifties and played on bomb sites.

 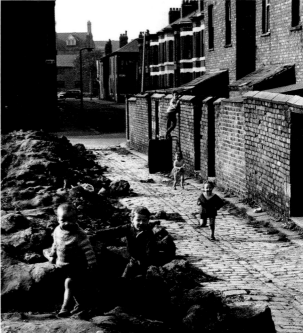

(Above left). Willie the singing Dalmatian does his stuff to his favourite song – Adam Faith's Baby. Willie was quite happy to go solo or sing along with the family. Three-year-old Ann Meroer who lived next door, was perhaps a little too young to appreciate Willie's greatness. Willie's owner, Mrs Florence Taylor of Beaufort Avenue, West Didsbury, said of Willie, "He only wants a guitar and he will really shake them".

(Above right). Lisa Kay says goodbye to Pip her pet white duck. For ever since Pip had been a ball of white fluff they had been together but now it was time to let go and Lisa had decided to donate Pip to Belle Vue Zoo. September 1968.

(Below). In 2017 this would be the stuff of health and safety nightmares, but back in February 1965 it seemed perfectly normal to put little Lisa Roland in with Belle Vue Zoo's baby elephant. Both were thirteen months old.

The World of Work

During the 1940s and 50s, NCB Mosley Common Colliery underwent what was in effect a complete rebuild, including widening the diameter of the main shaft by ten feet and installing the world's largest electric-driven winding engine.

NCB Bedford Colliery, Leigh, on 20 September 1966. The colliery employed 518 underground and 131 surface workers. When Bedford Colliery closed in 1967, the coal industry in Lancashire employed about 31,000 workers. Of its output, 44.6per cent went to electricity generation, 27.2per cent to industry, 15.8per cent for domestic use, 8.8per cent to gas, 2.9per cent for collieries use and just 0.7per cent to the railways. (Clive Hardy)

(Above) Agecroft Colliery closed in the 1930s though shafts No.3 and No.4 were retained for pumping nearby collieries. During the summer of 1951, the NCB undertook a series of test borings that indicated Agecroft had 80million tonnes of workable reserves. Work began in 1953 on a £9million programme to rehabilitate the colliery. The old No.3 and No.4 shafts were retained for further use and a new 2000ft deep 24ft diameter shaft (No.5) was sunk.

Our image from 1960 was probably taken several weeks before the first coal was brought to the surface. The tall structure that dominates the picture is the Keope-type friction winding tower above No.5 shaft. The colliery's main customer was the nearby CEGB Agecroft Power Station, the coal transferred directly by means of an enclosed conveyor belt.

(Left) The lamp room.

Knocking-off time at Trafford Park on a winter's evening in February 1966. Many people still used bicycles as their means of getting to and from work. Car ownership was increasing. The top selling car for 1966 was the Ford Cortina. The Cortina II went into production during the year, selling for £669. The estate version cost £724.

Trafford Park from Buile Hill Park. In 1967 it was estimated that the firms on Trafford Park were providing about 50,000 jobs out of 90,000 in the Manchester-Salford-Trafford area.

(Left) Trafford Park had its own power station. (courtesy Manchester Libraries).

(Below) During the 1960s, the General Electric Company (GEC), under its dynamic chairman Arnold Weinstock, set about rationalizing the UK electrical industry through a series of mergers and aggressive take-overs. In 1967 GEC merged with AEI (Metrovick) and English Electric (a subsidiary of which was Vulcan Foundry at Newton-le-Willows). GEC also gained control of Lancashire Dynamo (pictured here) and Crypto. GEC then rationalized its Trafford Park operations which included closing AEI's Leonard Works and Lancashire Dynamo. In all 10,000 jobs went. (R E Stanley, courtesy Manchester Libraries).

(Opposite page top) A Manchester Liner discharges grain at Brown & Polson's wharf, Trafford Park, in September 1969. When Brown & Polson extended their site at Trafford Park, they also acquired the old Guinness Wharf. Their first cargo of maze was landed there during September 1956.

(Opposite page bottom) The *Manchester Port* (8938 gross tons) at Manchester Dry Docks. Delivered in November 1966, she was capable of handling traditional break-bulk cargoes and standard containers of the day which were 20ft long. Her engines were a French design built under licence by Crossley at Openshaw. Containerisation took off during the late 1960s and initially many shipping companies converted existing cargo liners as a temporary measure until new purpose-built ships were available. (Courtesy Manchester Libraries).

(Below). The *Manchester Shipper* (7881grt) joined the fleet in 1943. After the war she was one of the first ships in the merchant navy to be fitted with radar, enabling her to navigate the St Lawrence in conditions that forced other vessels to stop. During 1961, she was used for some of the location filming for the screen adaptation of Salford playwright Shelagh Delaney's *A Taste of Honey*. *Manchester Shipper* was sold for breaking up in 1969. The reason she survived so long was probably due to her being fitted with a 30ton derrick, enabling her to handle the large containers favoured by the Americans.

(Opposite page top) The new *Manchester City* was visited by Manchester's Deputy Mayor, Alderman R C Rodgers as she prepared to make her maiden voyage to the USA and Canada. The *Manchester Evening News* ran the following piece on her titled 'New 'TV ship' has mod cons'. 'Built for Manchester Liners, on the Tees, this 17-knot cargo vessel is one of the first remote-controlled ships in Britain. The captain not only has full control from the wheelhouse of the main engine, he can also 'see' the engine-room and cargo holds by closed circuit television. The closed-circuit TV will be used as a navigation aid when the ship is negotiating the Manchester Ship Canal and the St Lawrence Seaway to help reduce the possibility of contact damage. A camera with a wide-angle lens suspended 40 feet above the main deck will give an unobscured picture of any activity ahead of the ship and on the fo'c'sle head. The *Manchester City*, which has a crew of 39 and will be commanded by Captain John E Jones, of Wolverhampton, is the third vessel owned by the company to bear this name'.

(Opposite page bottom) All quiet along No.9 Dock at Manchester on 16 May 1966, as the first national strike called by the National Union of Seamen since 1911 begins. The strike for higher wages and a reduction in the working week from 56 to 40 hours was widely supported by members, and by 1 June, nearly 20,000 seafarers were out. Ships at sea worked normally, their crews only going on strike when they returned to their home port. Strike pay was £3 a week, which wasn't too bad for a teenager like myself as my merchant navy pay at the time was £24 a month.

(Below) Ships laid up at Manchester on 29 June 1966, during the Seamen's Strike. The Manchester Liners vessels in the previous picture, have been moved from No.9 Dock to berths along Trafford Wharf, and Nos.6 and 7 Docks. Ray Gunter, the Minister of Labour, acknowledged that merchant navy pay and conditions needed modernising. Prime Minister Harold Wilson criticised the strikers, declaring the union had been taken over by Communists and that their aim was to bring down his administration. A state of emergency was declared. There was a cap on food prices to stop profiteering. Very quickly ports such as Liverpool, Southampton and London became congested with idle ships. The Royal Navy was authorised to take control and move vessels to clear berths.

During the 1960s, the advent of containerisation of goods was perhaps the most important change in the way cargoes were handled and carried. At Manchester, a container terminal was built on the north side of No.9 Dock. For a few years, containerisation traffic prospered with the value of goods passing through increasing year-on-year even if it fell by volume.

However, the need to accommodate more and more containers led to bigger and bigger containerships. This would disadvantage Manchester Liners as the maximum length and beam of their vessels were restricted by the dimensions of the locks on the Ship Canal. October 1968.

Furness Withy's 9442grt *Pacific Northwest* enters Mode Wheel Locks in December 1967. She was on an outward voyage from Manchester carrying general cargo for west coast ports of the USA and Canada.

The 7419grt *Clan Macilwrath* makes her way along the Manchester Ship Canal. Four of her five holds were forward of the engine room. *Clan Macilwrath* and her sistership, *Clan Macindoe*, were the only Clan Line vessels each equipped with three bipod masts.

(Left) On 16 March 1969, the *Manchester Courage* (12039 gross tons) departed No.9 Dock later than scheduled due to engine problems. As the Courage approached Irlam Lock, a hydraulic system failure caused her variable pitch propeller to move to forward thrust mode and the vessel rammed the lock gates, ending up wedged half in, half out. The water level between Irlam and Barton locks dropped. Manchester Docks were effectively cut off from the sea to all shipping, apart from vessels drawing less than nine or ten feet of water. The plan was that such vessels might be able to use the smaller undamaged parallel lock normally used by tugs. Fifteen vessels were trapped in Manchester, the estimated time for repairs being six to eight weeks. The cargo aboard Manchester Courage was offloaded using a giant crane and sent to Liverpool by road, where it was put onto a chartered containership.

(Below) The Ashton Canal at Ancoats. All traffic on the canal had ceased by 1958 and by the time this image was taken c1962 it was close to being unnavigable. The Inland Waterways Association campaigned to reopen it and the section through Droylsden was cleared in 1968. (T Brooks, courtesy Manchester Libraries).

(Above). The Rochdale Canal between Deansgate and Oxford Street, c1960. The section between the Bridgewater and Ashton Canals remained useable, even if the odd hazard to navigation existed. Further north, the canal had been closed to public navigation following the granting of an act of parliament. The possibility that the canal might reopen was not considered by the planners of the M62 motorway, as its construction cut the waterway in two.

(Below). The Rochdale Canal near Castlefields, c1960. (Both images courtesy Manchester Libraries).

(Above) Facing an uncertain future on 23 April 1963. Some of Gorton's 1400 workers gather to watch as the last locomotive to be overhauled at the works is readied for departure. On 31 May, the last 400 men were laid off and the works closed for good. Only a handful would again find work requiring similar skills and many drifted into lesser paid jobs. Many of those aged over sixty never worked again.

One former worker had eight jobs in nine years including toilet attendant with British Steel, crane driver, window cleaner, and labourer in a print works. Eventually his parish priest from St Vincent's, Openshaw, offered him a job as caretaker at the church school. When interviewed by *Evening News* reporter Brian Hope in 1972, John Smith had been school caretaker for seven years.

(Left) The boiler shop at Gorton was still busy in September 1962. A few months later the place would be empty.

By 1964 the commercial locomotive builder, Beyer, Peacock & Co, Gorton, was struggling. The workforce, which in 1950 had been 1934 strong, had been reduced to 556. New orders for the company's powerful articulated steam locomotives had dried up, forcing the company into a massive reorganisation programme. It entered several joint ventures to build diesel and electric locomotives. Between 1960-62, the company collaborated with Metropolitan-Vickers to build ten electric locomotives for British Rail's west coast services. A joint venture with Bristol Siddeley Engines resulted in a contract from British Rail Western Region for 101 diesel-hydraulic locomotives for use on main line services. Peacock also won a sub-contract order from Clayton Equipment to build twenty-nine centre-cab 900hp diesel electrics also for British Rail. Despite these orders, it wasn't enough to keep the company going.

In desperation, they contracted during 1964 to build fifty-four 1250hp diesel-electrics for British Rail at a loss in the hope that something else might turn up. It didn't. What did turn up were three new board members, a new chairman, and a new policy. All production was to end at the Gorton Foundry. Only thirty-six of the 1250hp locos were completed at Gorton, the remainder were built by BR Derby. With hindsight, it is possible that the company could have built these locos for a profit. Theirs was the only batch of the entire class offered to a commercial builder. It is thought that the order was placed with Peacock to give the company a lifeline. (T Bowker, courtesy Manchester Libraries).

The bogie shop at Beyer, Peacock & Co, Gorton, 1966. (T Bowker, courtesy Manchester Libraries).

Hydraulic press, Beyer, Peacock & Co, Gorton, 1966. (T Bowker, courtesy Manchester Libraries).

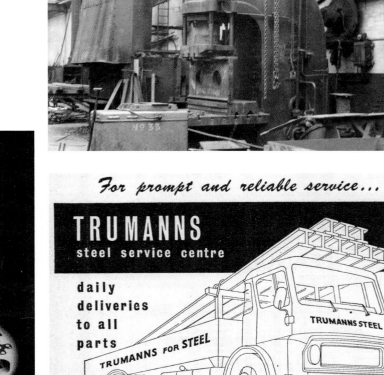

A highly successful company that built locomotives for domestic and overseas customers, Vulcan Foundry at Newton-le-Willows became part of the English Electric group in 1957. Newton-le-Willows built nearly 1000 diesel and electric locomotives for British Rail including the 22-strong Deltic class. These diesel-electrics were designed to replace the Eastern Region's streamlined steam locomotives that had been the mainstay of their fast, east coast mainline expresses since the 1930s. Completed during 1961-62, the Deltics, named after the Napier Deltic power plant that enabled them to reach service speeds of 100mph, were for their size, the most powerful diesel-electric locomotives in the world. They were purchased by BR under a service contract, English Electric carrying out maintenance and overhauls. Additional Deltic power plants were manufactured to allow fast engine changes. In 1963 a Deltic-hauled Flying Scotsman service made a record-breaking run of 5hours 55minutes from Kings Cross to Edinburgh including a stop at Newcastle.

This picture, taken at Thomas W Ward's scrapyard, Ducie Road, Salford, in February 1966, shows what looks like a steam locomotive being broken up. It is in fact English Electric's 2700hp experimental gas-turbine powered loco GT3. Built in 1961, GT3 was trialled by BR as a possible replacement for steam traction. Despite it performing well, BR decided to stick with diesels, and GT3 was returned to the Vulcan Foundry. Ironically it was towed to Wards by a steam loco.

At the beginning of the 1960s, the Avro plant at Woodford was building Mk 2 Vulcan bombers for the RAF. The earlier Vulcans had been designed to drop free-fall nuclear weapons. The Mk 2 was different. It was designed to carry the Blue Steel stand-off nuclear weapon, in effect an early cruise missile which could be released 100 miles from the target. The first Mk 2 made its maiden flight on 19 August 1958 and was delivered to the RAF's 230 OCU (operational conversion unit) on 1 July 1960. Our image shows a Mk 2 flying over the crowd at the Farnborough Air Show in September 1960.

On 1 July 1963, Avro became part of the Hawker Siddeley Aviation Group. Avro had already taken the decision to re-enter the civil aviation market and had designed the Avro 748, a medium-sized turboprop airliner carrying 40 passengers that could use short-field and regional airports. The first production 748 flew on 30 August 1961, entering service with Skyways Airways a few months later. Under Hawker Siddeley, the aircraft was designated the HS 748 and over the years the design went through several variants – the Series 2, 2A and 2B, that allowed for the fitting of more powerful engines, as well as a large forward freight door in the 2A and 2B variants.

A pair of HS 748s cross during an air show at Biggin Hill in 1964.

(Above) Queen Elizabeth II pays a visit to Mather & Platt in March 1965. The company were mechanical, electrical, hydraulic and fire suppression engineers, manufacturing a wide range of equipment ranging from steel roller shutters to flameproof motors and from Thermolier unit heaters to the Mulsifyre extinguisher system for supressing oil fires.

(Below). Throughout the 1950s Textile Machinery Makers (TMM) remained Platt Brothers (Holdings) largest subsidiary. Originally formed in 1931 when Platt Brothers; Asa Lees & Co; Brooks & Doxey; Dobson & Barlow; Joseph Hibbert; John Hetherington & Sons and Howard & Bullough exchanged their textile machinery assets for shares in the new venture though all continued to trade under their individual names. However, the Sixties was a decade of rapid change for the industry and demand for textile machinery was falling. In October 1962, Rochdale was rocked with the announcement that due to a drop in the demand for spinning machinery, Tweedales & Smalley (a wholly owned subsidiary of Platt Brothers since 1957), would close its Globe Works at the end of the year with the loss of 1600 jobs. TMM underwent a root and branch reorganisation that led in 1970 to the formation of Platt International.

Textile machine manufacturers Arundel-Coulthard, Chestergate, Stockport, had been a pleasant place to work with no history of worker dissatisfaction or trade union militancy. All that changed in July 1965 when the company was bought for £500,000 by Roberts Co, Sandforth, South Carolina. The firm changed its name to Roberts-Arundel and the new boss, Robert E Pomeranz, believed the only good employee was one who did exactly as he was told. Trouble soon erupted and workers began taking industrial action.

On 17 November 1966, the company made some of its male employees redundant and took on its first female workers. Pomeranz refused point blank to discuss the women's terms and conditions with the union, the AEU. Less than a fortnight later, Pomeranz took on more female employees, sacked every one of his 145 male workers and advertised for non-union labour. What had been a local strike was now set to become one of the longest industrial disputes in the history of the British trade union movement.

There was a daily picket of the works and the AEU organised a boycott of Roberts-Arundel goods. Firms that continued to do business with Roberts-Arundel were themselves blacklisted. On 22 February 1967, somewhere between 1000 and 2000 workers from around the Stockport area marched on the factory entrance. The mood was getting ugly and the chief constable threatened to read the Riot Act. Under the Act, a gathering of twelve or more people could be declared an unlawful assembly, and those so assembled given one hour to disperse. The law could then use any means necessary to disperse the assembly. Anyone assisting in the dispersal was indemnified against any legal consequences. One of the most notorious uses of the Act had been at Peterloo in 1819.

Talks were hastily arranged but collapsed after Pomeranz said, "There is no harm in talking, but I would urge the unions to find new jobs for their members". A second march took place on 21 March and the dispute continued to escalate. Questions were asked in the House of Commons. The boycott of Roberts-Arundel spread worldwide. When 30,000 workers across the North West came out in sympathy, the Tory press was convinced it was all a Communist plot.

By January 1968, Roberts-Arundel was financially crippled, yet Pomeranz refused to negotiate, even after other Stockport area employers offered to find temporary jobs for the strikers until the firm could re-employ them. Pomeranz announced the factory would close, but some strikers continued to picket until it was put up for sale.

Benson's Mill, Droylsden. The driving force behind the government's Cotton Industry Act 1959 was an attempt to save the industry through modernisation, closures and amalgamation. Manufacturers were encouraged to re-equip with modern machinery and take advantage of the latest technical innovations. The estimates for scrapping out-of-date spinning, doubling and weaving machinery was put at £11million – about £231million in 2017 prices. Re-equipping with the latest machinery was estimated at £19million – about £399million in 2017. For spinning alone, Oldham, once the largest cotton spinning town in the world, would lose 26 mills and 1,755,526 spindles.

The decline continued throughout Lancashire and mills continued to close at the rate of one a week, despite an influx of workers from the Indian sub-continent that enabled mill owners to move to round-the-clock production. During the mid-1960s one section of the textile industry to see growth was the outdoor trade (rucksacks, tents, sleeping bags, clothing). The growing popularity for camping and outdoor pursuits saw the turnover of leading UK manufacturers grow. (T Brooks, courtesy Manchester Libraries)

Bowker Bank Dye Works, Crumpsall, c1966. (L H Price, courtesy Manchester Libraries).

(Left) Cotton Board Show, January 1961. Model Jennifer Lejeune sports a multi-coloured striped sun-suit and raffia sombrero-type hat.

(Above) Shelagh Wilson on her last assignment as a model prior to retiring from the catwalk to concentrate on running her Manchester-based modelling agency.

(Right) In 1963, fashion designer Mary Quant (in centre of the girls) launched her Ginger Group wholesale design and manufacturing company, offering up-to-date lines at affordable prices. Quant is often considered the inventor of miniskirt: she certainly popularised it and gave it its name, though some fashion historians think John Bates was the originator. Bates' designs featured short hemlines and as early as 1962 he was experimenting with PVC clothing. He also designed Diana Rigg's outfits for her role as Mrs Peel in *The Avengers*. Our image dates from 10 February 1966, when Quant and her Ginger Group were holding a fashion show at Lewis's store, Market Street, Manchester. It was also the year Quant launched her cosmetics range. Three years later, Quant popularised a new fashion craze – hot pants. Though Mary influenced female fashion, it was the Beatles who influenced young men's fashion with mop haircuts, collarless jackets and Cuban-heeled boots.

(Above left) Dresses made by Manchester based companies were on show in February 1968, prior to their inclusion in a sales drive of UK textiles and clothing lines to West Germany. Four-year-old Sharon Evans, of Chadderton, and 19-year-old Jane Powell do the modelling.

(Above right) New Courtaulds' fabrics for 1970 went on show during November 1969, including this tricel jersey that was expected to retail for £6.6s.0d. At the time Courtaulds was on the rise; from man-made fibre producer, to the world's largest textile manufacturer. In 1962 they had proposed that the Lancashire Cotton Co, English Sewing Cotton Co, Fine Spinners & Doublers, Tootals, and Combined English Mills (Spinners) join with them in a new company. However, agreement was not reached though they did acquire Fine Spinners & Doublers in 1963 and the Lancashire Cotton Board in 1964. These two acquisitions gave Courtaulds control of around 30per cent of Lancashire's spinning capacity.

(Left) Manchester United star George Best and Manchester City's Mike Summerbee at the opening of Best's fashion boutique in Manchester in September 1967. Openshaw-born Davy Jones of The Monkees pop group also entered the world of retail fashion, opening Zich in Greenwich Village, New York. The Sixties was the decade when, for the first time, teenagers had fashion shops catering solely to their tastes.

The latest recruits to the bowler hat brigade in October 1962 were these Manchester binmen. They had taken to wearing the bowlers they had discovered abandoned outside an office in New Market Street.

Facebook Memories

Christina McGraw – I worked at C&A, great priced clothes. I also liked Wallis. I have a 60s coat from there, perfect condition. Just too tight for me.

Alan Grundy – I worked for a company called Customagic in the 60s. We took over an old sewing factory on Pin Mill Brow in Ardwick, Manchester. In the workrooms we found Mary Quant dress labels for the Ginger Group range of garments. It is now the site of a PC World clearance outlet. This humble factory helped give birth to a fashion revolution.

Sandra Mason – I was working in Lewis's (when Mary Quant was in Manchester) and the manager couldn't understand what all the fuss was about! She was very straight-laced and didn't think girls should wear mini-skirts and dresses.

Glynis Kennear – I didn't work in the rag trade but my wedding dress was a Mary Quant. Velvet with white chiffon sleeves. Beautiful. Wish I had kept it.

Fran Butcher – I worked at Tootals on Oxford Road. Office Junior. Learnt quite a lot there. Was asked to do some fashion sketches for an in-house magazine.

Dustmen march on the Town Hall, Manchester, during an industrial dispute in October 1969. Later, Dick Pickering (check overcoat) appealed to the men to break up their gathering so that negotiations could reconvene inside.

Mrs Mabel McKennas gets to grips with some of the latest school cleaning equipment on offer in July 1966, including a Dixon New Regent floor dryer, a Dixon floor polisher and a VersaVac 250 vacuum cleaner – that's the dustbin-like thing on the left-hand side of the image.

Chimney sweep Fred Gibson on his round in Chadderton. 1965.

On the move?

By November 1965, work on the second stage of the £5.3million Mancunian Way was running behind schedule due to problems encountered when sinking the supporting piles. A geological fault – the West Manchester Fault – runs practically parallel to Oxford Road, resulting in the piles on one side of Mancunian Way having to be sunk to a greater depth than originally planned. Our picture was taken from the roof of what was then the John Dalton College of Technology, Chester Street.

(Above left) Research student Mike Berresford, of Salford University Transport Studies Department, monitors traffic flows on Mancunian Way, June 1969.

(Above right) Mancunian Way where it crosses over Upper Brook Street.

(Below) Fred Mulley, Minister of Transport, officially opening the thirteen-mile stretch of the M61 between Horwich and the Preston by-pass in December 1969.

Images from the aftermath of a pile-up on the M6 near Wigan during heavy fog in December 1969. The driver of a heavy-duty recovery vehicle takes a fag break whilst pondering how to prise these HGVs apart.

A second image from the same pile-up.

Weather chaos strikes Oldham as snow and ice on Manchester Road brings traffic almost to a standstill. November 1969.

Every motorist's nightmare, their car stalling in slow-moving traffic. It is Easter Bank Holiday, 7 April 1969, and holidaymakers are returning to Manchester along the A556. For those of you too young to remember, this is how most people started their car in the 1960s – with a few turns of the starting handle.

Someone who didn't need to use a starting handle was Manchester United star George Best, pictured here driving away in his Lotus Europa S2, one of the first of the type in the UK. George liked a drink, women and fast cars. He also owned an E-type Jaguar.

Considered by many to be the most popular car of the twentieth century, the Mk I Mini was introduced in 1959 and remained in production until 1967 when it was replaced by the Mk II. Designed by Alec Issigonis, the Mini was light, cheap to run and a steal at £497. Despite its size, Issigonis' radical design resulted in the Mini having more room inside than its predecessor, the Morris Minor. By 1965 more than one million had been sold and the car achieved international fame in 1969, when Minis were the getaway car of choice for Charlie Croker (Michael Caine) and his light-fingered lads in the movie *The Italian Job*.

Manchester United's David Herd working at his garage in Urmston in September 1967. He was on the mend after breaking a leg earlier in the year.

Joel Barnett, Labour MP for Heywood and Royton, meets the mums of Blackshaw Lane, Royton, who were fed up with having to manoeuvre prams around poorly sited road signs. The mums presented Joel with a petition and turned him loose with a pram so he could find out what it was like for himself.

Though car ownership was on the increase during the 1960s, many still relied on public transport for getting about. This image shows Ashton-under-Lyne Corporation No.29 (built by Leyland in 1962) on a Stalybridge service during the 1960s. Ashton was the last operator in the Manchester area to phase out its trolleybuses. Though the Houghton Green service had switched to motorbuses in July 1960, the next conversion did not take place until October 1964 with the Manchester via Guide Bridge route. Ashton's last trolleybus ran on 30 December 1966. (Clive Hardy)

The City of Manchester depot at Didsbury with a typical double-decker of the period. 3693 was built by Leyland in 1963 and was one of the last traditional back-loaders to be bought by the city. (Clive Hardy)

In the early 1960s Manchester acquired twenty Metropolitan-Cammell Daimler Fleetline rear-engined, front-loading double-deckers and these were quickly followed by 150 similarly configured Leyland Atlanteans. The Atlantean pictured here is Bolton Transport 265. Bolton ordered its first Atlanteans in 1963, though 265 is from a batch delivered in 1967. These new buses could easily be converted to one-man-operation with the driver collecting the fares, thereby doing the bus conductor out of a job. (Clive Hardy).

(Left). During late 1954, the domestic arm of British European Airways decided it wanted a slice of the action in the lucrative business passenger market between London and the North West. At the time, the fastest train took 3hrs 30min from city centre to city centre. The fastest BEA flight took 1hr 25min, added to which was the time it took at either end to get from the airport to city centre. BEA charged £3.17s.0d (£3.85p) one way, BR charged £2.0.3d (£2.2p) first-class. Nevertheless, BEA's service proved popular and within a couple of years it was carrying 60,000 passengers annually.

Not to be outdone, BR included the design and construction of a fleet of modern Pullman diesel-electric multiple units in its £1.2billion 1955 Modernisation Plan. On 23 June 1960, *Manchester Evening News* photographer John Fowler was at Central Station to photograph one of the six-car, first-class only, Midland Pullman sets. They were the first fully air-conditioned, sound-proofed trains to run on British Railways. As well as offering a level of passenger comfort far beyond anything then in service, the Pullmans were timed to run at 90mph non-stop. The service commenced on 5 July 1960.

On 18 April 1966, British Rail commenced scheduled electric services between Euston and the North West. Passenger numbers shot up and, by September, BR was showing increases of 84per cent for second-class and 43per cent for first-class. Not only was the new business retained, it continued to increase week on week. BR was giving the domestic airlines a run for their money. Worst hit was British Eagle's Liverpool – London services where passenger numbers fell by a half. BEA's Manchester – London route saw passenger numbers drop by a quarter. The Air Transport Licensing Board responded, allowing British Eagle to slash fares and introduce cheap standby returns. Not to be outdone, BR even had a go at tempting away BEA passengers flying to London Airport (Heathrow) to catch connecting flights by introducing a Watford Junction – London Airport express coach service.

The Queen and Prince Phillip leaving Manchester on 18 February 1965.

(Oppostie page and left this page) During the British Rail era, there were several railway accidents around the Greater Manchester area. On 28 May 1964, an excursion train carrying 250 schoolchildren to York was derailed at Cheadle Hulme, blocking both the Manchester-Crewe and Manchester-Macclesfield lines. The cause of the crash, in which three were killed and twenty injured including four seriously, was due to the train travelling at nearly 50mph over a temporary road bridge which had a 10mph speed restriction on it. The track burst and the bridge partially collapsed, causing the train to divide. The locomotive and four coaches cleared the platform, coming to a stand just beyond Cheadle Hulme signal box, though the rear of these coaches finished on its side. The remainder of the train was in the station, coaches wedged along the platform edge or stuck straddling the partially collapsed bridge. The driver had not been on the route for several months and had also missed speed restriction warning signs. The image at the bottom of the page opposite shows some of the children from the train at a nearby school awaiting evacuation from the scene.

(Below) January 1965, and the villagers of Strines are not happy bunnies. Evening trips into Manchester by train were impossible as the station closed every night at 7.30pm.

By early 1968, BR's surviving steam locomotives were concentrated around the northwest. Here a 2-8-0 freight locomotive wheezes its way through Manchester Victoria. (Clive Hardy)

(Above) Nearly three months after the end of steam, 2-8-0 No.48646 was at Bolton engine sheds probably waiting a tow to the scrapyard. (P Eckersley courtesy Clive Hardy).

(Right) On 11 August 1968, British Railways ran its last main line steam-hauled train, the Fifteen Guinea Special from Liverpool to Carlisle via Manchester and back. Our picture shows guard Henry Crossland blowing his whistle at 1106hrs for the train to depart Manchester Victoria for Carlisle. It was pulled by Britannia class Pacific No.70013 *Oliver Cromwell* – the last steam locomotive to be overhauled by BR. The following day, BR introduced a steam ban, though one locomotive was exempt. Due to contractual arrangements, the preserved steam locomotive *Flying Scotsman* could still venture out onto the main line.

Central station was opened by the Midland Railway on 1 July 1880. Its lack of any sort of façade led railway historian Hamilton Ellis to describe it as 'one of the most grandly desolate places of the kind in Great Britain'. The station's viability was first undermined in *The Reshaping of British Railways Report 1963*, by BRB chairman Richard Beeching, in which he proposed sweeping changes to the rail network. Though the report was based on evidence gathered from just one week's traffic receipts from 1961, and seriously flawed in other respects, something had to be done as British Rail's working deficit had risen from £16.5million in 1956 to a record £104million by 1962. The deficit was not all BR's fault – much of it could be laid at the feet of interfering politicians.

Loss-making passenger services were to be withdrawn. Beeching proposed closing 2128 stations to passenger traffic though many would remain open for goods and parcels. Manchester Central was not on the list, though it would be affected by a proposal to withdraw its passenger services to Sheffield Midland via Hope and to Derby via Chinley. The fate of Central and Exchange were in fact sealed by the *Duplicate Trunk Route Report of 1965*. Though not as well known to the public as Beeching, it was in many ways more far-reaching. This report called for some serious rationalisation. The closure of whole routes including major stations, while those that remained would be modernised or upgraded. Central and Exchange were subsequently approved for closure, both going on 5 May 1969. Another substantial station that closed was Stockport Tiviot Dale. During the early 1960s its services were gradually whittled away and it was closed completely on 2 January 1967.

On 6 March 1967, passenger services between Manchester Central and St Pancras via the Peak route were withdrawn. Minister of Transport Barbara Castle authorised the closure of Central Station providing its remaining services could be handled by Oxford Road and Piccadilly, and that Oxford Road was upgraded to handle an extra 10,000 passengers a day.

The work involved altering the track layout, providing an additional platform, covering over the footbridge, widening staircases, and upgrading former goods lifts to take passengers. A one-way traffic system was introduced on the station forecourt. Passengers using Oxford Road would be among the first outside London forced into adopting a tube mentality. As Oxford Road was all about squeezing a quart into a pint pot, trains were timed at less than one minute for platform duties to avoid delays.

(Above) Along with electrification of the west coast main line, British Rail's rebuilding of London Road Station had been scheduled to commence during 1959 but the money did not become available until 1963. The new station, renamed Piccadilly, was officially opened in May 1966. Our image dates from a couple of years later by which time the seven-storey Gateway House on the station approach had been completed.

Passengers off a BEA domestic flight arrive at rain-swept Manchester. It is November 1962, a time when BEA dominated the then most lucrative of the UK's internal routes. Even so, BEA recorded a loss of £2.1million on domestic operations for 1961-62, and £2.5million for 1962-63. Several airlines were involved in a turf war with British Rail for business passengers. Between 1960-66, BEA increased the number of flights on its Manchester – London, Manchester – Glasgow routes, from 50 and fourteen respectively, to 68 and eighteen. By employing larger aircraft, BEA doubled the number of seats it could offer per week in both directions, from 3500 to 7750 on the London route and from 658 to 1260 on its Glasgow service.

In March 1966, BEA chairman, Anthony Milward, said that he expected the main battle for passengers would be on the London route. So, what were the comparisons between air and rail then like? Well, if you were going to London to connect with another flight, BEA won hands down. However, if you were doing a city centre to city centre journey, it was worth doing a few sums. By April 1966, the fastest you could do it by plane, including taxi or coach journeys, was 160min.

BEA charged £6.13s.0d (£6.65p) one way including the coach fare. An ordinary return by air cost £9.14s.0d (£9.70p), though cheap deals were around at £5.18s.0d (£5.90p). British Rail's all first-class Midland Pullman ran non-stop to London; the single fare being £4.19s.9d (£4.95p). A second class return Manchester – London would set you back £5.0s.0d, though cheap day returns were £2.17s.0d (£2.85p). For those of you with money to burn, British Rail offered a first-class sleeper service at the single fare of £5.14s.9d (£5.75p).

In the early 1960s, facilities were still somewhat Spartan. This is passport control, though with the canvas-seat chairs, the décor might easily be mistaken for a doctor's waiting room. Times were changing. During 1962, the Duke of Edinburgh officially opened a new terminal and control tower block.

This is the redoubtable Mrs Amy Crossley, who at 81 was still pulling a shift in the airport restaurant. During quiet spells, Mrs Crossley kept fit using the flex from the vacuum cleaner as a skipping rope. We believe the picture was taken in September 1963.

Freight handling at Manchester in 1969. In 1950 the airport handled about 14,900tonnes of freight but advances in handling techniques and palletisation brought a substantial increase in traffic. By the end of the decade, the airport was handling more than 40,000tonnes of freight a year.

7 July 1964, and Gerry Marsden of Gerry and the Pacemakers is pictured on a break during location filming for *Ferry 'Cross the Mersey*. In the film, Gerry and the boys play art students whose big break as musicians comes when they win a talent contest. However, disaster looms when they discover that their instruments have mistakenly been sent to the airport. Gerry wrote nine songs for the movie, including *Ferry 'Cross the Mersey*. Also appearing were Cilla Black, The Fourmost, and Julie Samuel.

The Rolling Stones arriving at Manchester from London. Left to right: Brian Jones, Bill Wyman, Keith Richards, Mick Jagger and Charlie Watts.

Manchester United on their way to play Racing Club Strasbourg in the Inter Cities Fairs Cup 4th Round, May 1965.

One of the major developments at Manchester during the 1960s was the runway extension. The new length of 2745metres enabled fully laden aircraft to take off and fly non-stop to Canada.

The British Midland Canadair C4-Argonaut G-ALHG photographed a few weeks before the Stockport air disaster. A problem with her fuel system had been logged five days before the crash.

On 4 June 1967, British Midland Canadair C4 Argonaut G-ALHG, chartered by Arrowsmith Holidays, took off from Palma de Mallorca for Ringway, with 79 passengers and a crew of five. On the approach to Ringway, Captain Harry Marlow was unable to line the plane up with the extended runway centreline and called an overshoot, meaning he would go around again and make a second attempt at landing. It was during this second approach that things went disastrously wrong. As the aircraft flew over Stockport, the two starboard wing engines suddenly cut out and the aircraft became uncontrollable. It was the stuff of aviation nightmares. An airliner crashing into a densely-populated area. However, the aircraft avoided a gasometer and a block of flats, crashing at 1009hrs on the small, open area of Hopes Carr.

Although there were no fatalities on the ground, 72 of those on board the Argonaut died, and not all of them quickly. Within minutes the wreckage was engulfed in flames. Passengers at the front of the aircraft had died because of the impact but others were trapped in their seats and were burnt to death. Rescuers were soon on the scene. Police constables John Heath and Bill Oliver, along with civilians Brian Quinn and Brian Donohoe, helped in the rescue of twelve seriously injured survivors.

The Accident Investigation Branch (AIB) report makes interesting reading. It found that the reason No's 3 and 4 engines cut out was due to fuel starvation due to a leaky valve caused by a design error. A fuel problem with this same aircraft had been noted just five days before the crash, though this fact did not become known until the following October. Though the aircraft was fitted with a fuel warning alarm, it was impossible for the crew to hear it unless they happened to be leaning forward when it went off. This was impossible, as shoulder straps on their seats prevented them from doing so.

The investigation also found that the bracing bars holding the seats in place were too weak to survive a crash impact, causing the rows to concertina into one another and trapping people who might otherwise have survived.

The grim task of searching through the wreckage.

These two images give us some idea of just how close to the built-up area of Stockport the plane came. News reports at the time stated that the pilot, Captain Harry Marlow, chose to crash in an open area but the AIB found no evidence to support this. With two engines out of action, the AIB believed the aircraft was uncontrollable due to loss of power.

Captain Marlow could not recall the sequence of events and his first officer had died in the crash. Witnesses said that moments before coming down, the plane had made a pronounced turn to port and levelled out.

The AIB interpreted this as Captain Marlow and his first officer attempting to regain control at critically slow speed, and that Captain Marlow had managed to exert enough control at the critical moment for the plane to come down where it did. The AIB rightly absolved Captain Marlow of all blame.

Air hostess Jane Timson was the sole survivor of this crash at Manchester Airport on 20 March 1969. The BEA Viscount had just taken off on a routine training flight, when it suddenly plunged into the runway.

Facebook Memories

John Roberts – I can remember flying out of Manchester Airport with my family when I was a young lad. It was a package holiday and our first trip abroad. We were so excited! I'm pretty sure we were on an old Britannia which seemed to take ages to get there.

Michael Green – Catching the school bus every day used to big adventure when we were young. I remember the smog being so bad sometimes that Mum used to make us wear our scarves over our mouths. The first we saw of the bus was two headlights coming out of the fog.

People and Places

(Left) Market Street in its pre-Arndale days. A Corporation tower lorry has been pressed into service to help with the erection of Christmas 1962 street decorations. The cameraman is standing with his back to Spring Gardens. In the distance is the relatively new Marks & Spencer store. The buildings housing Timpson Shoes and John Collier were among those demolished for the Arndale development.

(Below) The Kardomah coffee shop chain was an integral part of the British high street from the Edwardian era, with Manchester having at least three outlets. In 1962 the chain was sold to the Forte Group and though Kardomahs became popular with Mods during the mid-1960s, the brand lost its appeal and branches began closing. Our image shows the Market Street outlet.

(Above) The Marks & Spencer store on Market Street was completed in the early 1960s and was instantly recognisable due to its unique wave form canopy. A school leaver taking a job as a junior sales assistant could expect to earn £2.10s.0d to £3.0s.0d a week for a 40hour week depending on the company they worked for.

The calm before the storm. Customers gather at the bakery and cakes counter at Lewis's store, Manchester. The bakers are on strike but the word on the street is that a delivery is on the way.

Tory leader Edward Heath does a spot of Christmas shopping in Manchester before heading off to Piccadilly station to catch his train back home. December 1969.

On the stump at Alexander Park, Manchester, in October 1960, is none other than Sir Oswald Moseley. In the late-1940s he founded the Union Movement whose aim was a united Europe. As with his British Union of Fascists in the 1930s, Moseley's Union Movement meetings often ended in violence. Moseley eventually moved to Ireland and later to France, returning to the UK in the wake of the Notting Hill race riots. He stood in the 1959 general election as the Union Movement candidate for Kensington North and lost his deposit. His last attempt at regaining a seat in parliament came in the 1966 general election when he stood for Shoreditch and Finsbury and polled 1126 votes.

Prime Minister Harold Wilson officially opens the Mancunian Way. During 1967-68, Wilson's government allocated £225million for road building and legislation governing the use of seat belts, breathalyser tests, lorry drivers' hours and an experimental 70mph speed limit. The Transport Act 1968 also provided funds to authorities maintaining passenger services if justified on social grounds.

(Left) Prime Minister Sir Alec Douglas-Home visits the Bear Pit, Stockport, whilst on the campaign trail for the 1964 general election. As the 14th Earl of Home, he was serving as Foreign Secretary when Harold Macmillan resigned due to a prostate condition. On 23 October 1963, he renounced his peerage becoming Sir Alec Douglas-Home thereby enabling him to contest – and win – the Kinross and West Perthshire seat. As Prime Minister, Sir Alec led the country for just 363 days, the second shortest premiership of the twentieth century. The general election of October 1964 returned Labour to power under Harold Wilson with a four-seat majority.

Irish MP Bernadette Devlin at Manchester University. A civil-rights activist, she won the seat for Mid-Ulster at a by-election in 1969, becoming at the time the youngest MP and the youngest woman to be elected to Westminster. Though a Republican Socialist, she took the Oath of Allegiance so she could represent her constituents. In December 1969, she was convicted and jailed for incitement to riot during the Battle of the Bogside. Re-elected in 1970, she then sat as an Independent Socialist.

In August 1969, the tensions between Republican and Loyalist communities finally erupted into bloody violence and sixteen people died during the rioting that followed the annual Protestant and Unionist Apprentice Boys' Parade.

The Irish Civil Rights Solidarity Campaign was based in Manchester and Manchester students set up the Civil Rights Committee. These were not sectarian organisations and fought for rights of Protestants and Catholics alike. The Campaign for Social Justice (CSJ) had been formed in Northern Ireland by Patricia McCluskey in 1964 to fight discrimination against Catholics in Ulster, especially over housing.

In October 1969, Tory controlled Manchester City Council refused to allow the CSJ to hold public meetings in council-owned halls. On 6 November, a torchlit procession made its way through the city centre and a coffin and wreath to the death of free speech were laid on the steps of Manchester Town Hall.

(Left) Anti-apartheid protestors outside the South African Airways offices in Peter Street in November 1969. Manchester police officers at the scene said that no arrests would be made providing the protestors did not obstruct the pavement.

(Below) Students from Didsbury College of Education march to the Department of Education, Crown Square, Manchester, in December 1969, in solidarity with teachers who were demanding a pay rise to take their pay to a minimum of £13.0s.0d a week.

(Right) HRH Prince Phillip at his inauguration as Chancellor at Salford University in 1967, an appointment he would hold until 1991. His robes were embroidered with symbols depicting science and nuclear energy.

(Below) Manchester University Rag Week 1969 had a medieval touch about it. Manchester's rag weeks were consistently at the top when it came to raising money for good causes.

(Left) Soviet cosmonaut Yuri Gagarin (the first man to go into space) seen here with Sir Bernard Lovell (Jodrell Bank) at Manchester Town Hall, July 1961. Gagarin became an overnight international sensation following his Vostok 1 mission of 12 April 1961, and was sent on a worldwide tour to promote the USSR's achievement. The flight took the US completely by surprise and John F Kennedy set NASA the goal of a manned flight by the end of the decade. In 1963 Valentina Tereshkova became the first female cosmonaut to go into space.

(Below) When completed in 1957, the 250ft diameter mark 1 telescope at Jodrell Bank was the largest steerable radio telescope in the world. During the 1950s and 60s, both the USA and USSR asked for Jodrell Bank's assistance in tracking various satellites and space probes. It was the only piece of kit capable of confirming that the USSR's Sputnik 1's booster rocket had fired. During the Cuban Missile Crisis, the telescope was discreetly pointed eastward acting as an early-warning radar should the Soviets launch their missiles. The telescope was only expected to have a life span of ten years and, as the sixties wore on, signs of fatigue began to show. However, such had been the success of Jodrell Bank that £400,000 was allocated for repairs and upgrades which were carried out between 1968 and 1971.

Albert Square in 1967. Approval had been given to turn the square into a tree-filled plaza. Mature trees 30-35ft tall were to be brought in and planted in the central reservation and on the broad pavement in front of the Town Hall.

In June 1958, the first parking meters in the UK were installed along Mayfair, London; the charge being 6d (2.5p) for one hour. Our image, taken during the installation of trees along the central reservation, shows the meters bagged. Parking meters featured in the 1967 movie *Cool Hand Luke*, starring Paul Newman. Newman's character gets banged up for decapitating parking meters. The film sparked copycat meter decapitations throughout the UK.

The Rylands Building was built in 1929-32 as a textile warehouse, though its design incorporated provisions for retail outlets on the ground and first storeys. Among those renting space were Marks & Spencer, who took up most of the corner on High Street and Dolcis Shoes who had their shop on the corner of Tib Street. Our image is from the 1960s when much of the building was occupied by Pauldens Department Store. Pauldens moved in following the destruction by fire of their Stretford Road premises in 1957. Photographs of the fire are featured in our companion book, *Around Manchester in the 1950s*.

(Above) Two images featuring the Royal Exchange in the early 1960s. The trading floor was still open for business, although the cotton trade was in decline. When King George V officially opened the new extension in 1921, more than 2000 firms were represented here and there were more than 11,000 members. By 1968 there were so few members left that the exchange was no longer considered viable. Some, though by no means all, had gone to the wall and others had amalgamated into larger organisations. Up on the roof in June 1960, scientific assistant Dinah Sutcliffe demonstrates one of the new rainfall gauges that had been installed.

Across the rooftops. Looking north west from St Andrews House c1965.
(Courtesy Manchester Libraries).

This view across the rooftops of Salford and Manchester dates from July 1964. The CIS tower block, Miller Street, is the tall building in the left background. It was designed by G S Hay and Sir John Burnet Tait and Partners to provide no less than thirteen acres of office accommodation on 25 floors, over a five-storey podium. When completed in 1962, it was, at 400ft tall, the highest office building in Europe.

Across the rooftops. Looking toward Salford c1962. (Courtesy Manchester Libraries).

Third Avenue, Trafford Park. (T Brooks, courtesy Manchester Libraries).

This is 459 Third Avenue at the junction with Second Street, Trafford Park. (T Brooks, courtesy Manchester Libraries).

382-408 Stockport Road, Longsight, looking towards Daisy Bank. (W Kay, courtesy Manchester Libraries).

Stockport from the railway viaduct. Portwood cooling tower is in the centre of the image and the gasometer is partially hidden behind a grubby looking St Mary's Parish Church. The bus depot and offices are just beyond and to the left of Wellington bridge. Some initial demolition appears to be under way for the Merseyway Shopping Centre. (Clive Hardy)

The first survivors of the Stockport Air Disaster to leave hospital were brothers Billy (12) and Harold Wood (14). They are pictured here saying goodbye to Sister Susan Butcher as they leave Stockport Infirmary. Their mum is the lady with the glasses.

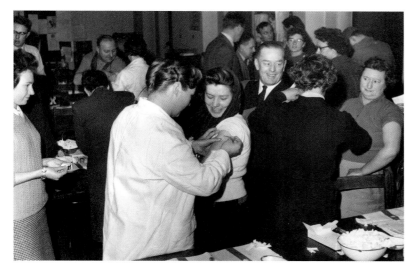

(Left) The first indications that Britain might be about to face an outbreak of smallpox emerged during December 1961 when several travellers arriving from Pakistan were suspected of carrying the virus. On 1 January 1962, one of the travellers was isolated in Bradford Fever Hospital. Ten days later the first case amongst Bradford's population was confirmed when a cook from the local Children's Hospital was admitted to the Fever Hospital. During January, smallpox broke out in the Rhondda – again the carrier was from Pakistan. The Rhondda had 25 confirmed cases resulting in six deaths. A massive vaccination programme was launched. Our image shows the scene at Manchester Town Hall.

(Right) A special oxygen chamber in use at Monsall Hospital, Manchester, November 1967. Patient Henry Marshall volunteered to go into the chamber for publicity purposes and he is seen here chatting to Sister Nora Sands. Also in the picture are Nurse Mary Chatterley and Cadet Elizabeth Wright. The chamber was one of the earliest to be equipped to play piped music to soothe the patient undergoing treatment.

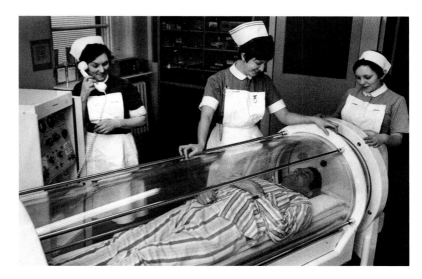

(Left) Nurses gather at the Albert Hall, Manchester, as part of an ongoing protest over salary scales. There were so many nurses there that traffic along Peter Street was at a standstill. The image dates from December 1969. It was a time when there was no disposable equipment – syringes etc., were reused. Bedpans were cleaned out and used from patient to patient. There were no heart monitors; no CPR; no computers. If a nurse was sitting at her work station when a doctor entered, she was expected to stand.

'ello 'ello 'ello. What's all this then? Well, it's New Year's Eve, December 1969, the clock is striking midnight and one of Manchester's finest is enjoying himself.

'Christmas is coming and the geese are getting fat'. Prisoners at Strangeways rehearse for their carol concert. It was the first year that the traditional tree had been replaced with a crib. December 1969.

Exercise time at Strangeways in August 1961. Though by this date the use of the death penalty was in decline, Strangeways would witness two more executions. On 28 November 1962, James Smith was executed for the murder of Mrs Sarah Isobella Cross in her corner sweetshop in Miles Platting. Miles Platting also featured in the second execution. It was where John Robson Walby, alias Gwynne Owen Evans, was arrested following a tip-off to Bolton police, on suspicion of murdering John Alan West at Seaton, Cumberland. West had been murdered by Walby and an accomplice during a robbery. Walby was executed on 13 August 1964. He was one of the last two people to be executed in England.

The Moors Murders

Ian Brady and Myra Hindley are responsible for one of the darkest episodes in what is now Greater Manchester. It began on 12 July 1963, when 16-year-old Pauline Reade disappeared on her way to a dance at the British Railway's Club, Gorton, and ended on 6 October 1965, when 17-year-old Edward Evans was enticed away from Manchester Central station. Between these events, Brady and Hindley were responsible for the disappearance of three more children: 12-year-old John Kilbride from Ashton-under-Lyne on 23 November 1963; 12-year-old Keith Bennett who vanished on his way to visit his grandmother on 16 June 1964, and 10-year-old Lesley Ann Downey who disappeared from a fairground on 26 December 1964. All five were murdered by Brady who also sexually assaulted at least four of them. Hindley claimed she had no part in the killings or sexual assaults, though Brady would later claim that she had murdered Lesley Ann Downey.

That Brady and Hindley were caught was due to Hindley's 17-year-old brother-in-law David Smith, who had convictions for burglary and actual bodily harm. Brady attempted to involve Smith in some way with Evans' murder.

Having picked up Evans, Brady and Hindley took the boy back to their home where they shared a bottle of wine. Brady then sent Hindley to fetch Smith. On their return, Hindley told her brother-in-law to wait outside and enter only when he saw a flashing light. Smith did as he was told and was shown into the kitchen by Brady who then left him there on the pretext of fetching wine.

A few minutes later there was a loud scream followed by Hindley bellowing from the living room for Smith to come and help. On entering, Smith saw Brady standing over the still screaming boy. Brady then struck Evans on the left side of his head using the flat of an axe. If that was not enough, Brady then throttled the boy with a length of electrical cord. Edward appears to have put up a struggle as Brady had sustained a sprained ankle and wanted Smith's help in disposing of the body. However, the boy's body was too heavy for Smith to carry out to Brady's car on his own so it was agreed that they would dispose of the corpse the following evening. In the meantime, it was trussed up in a plastic sheet.

After returning home, Smith told his wife everything. She told him that he must call the police and the following morning Smith did as he was told and contacted Hyde police station. Brady was arrested. On 11 October, Hindley was charged as an accessory to the murder of Edward Evans. Following a tip off from Smith, the police began a search of all left-luggage offices at Manchester stations. It was at Manchester Central that they found what they were looking for. Inside one of the suitcases were pornographic images of a young girl and a tape of her screaming and begging for help. It has been said that even the most hardened police officers found the tape difficult to listen to.

A search of Brady's house turned up dozens of photographs that appeared to have been taken on Saddleworth Moor. One hundred and fifty police officers were assigned to search the moor for locations that matched the images. It was another tip-off, this time from 11-year-old Pat Hodges, a neighbour of Brady and Hindley who had been with them on several trips to the moor, that led police to concentrate their search alongside the A635 road. On 16 October, police found the body of Lesley Ann Downey and five days later that of John Kilbride.

Police search outbuildings in the Charlestown area of Ashton-under-Lyne for missing John Kilbride. November 1963.

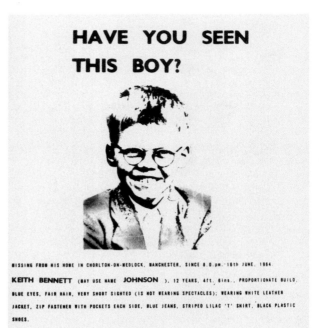

HAVE YOU SEEN THIS BOY?

MISSING FROM HIS HOME IN CHORLTON-ON-MEDLOCK, MANCHESTER, SINCE 8.0.pm.-16th JUNE, 1964.

KEITH BENNETT (MAY USE NAME **JOHNSON**), 12 YEARS, 4ft. 8ins., PROPORTIONATE BUILD. BLUE EYES, FAIR HAIR, VERY SHORT SIGHTED (IS NOT WEARING SPECTACLES); WEARING WHITE LEATHER JACKET, ZIP FASTENER WITH POCKETS EACH SIDE, BLUE JEANS, STRIPED LILAC 'T' SHIRT, BLACK PLASTIC SHOES.

ANY INFORMATION TELEPHONE CHIEF CONSTABLE, MANCHESTER CITY POLICE, CENTRAL 1212.

(Above left) Winifred Bennett (left), mother of Keith Bennett, pictured with her daughter Margaret, talking to Mrs Sheila Kilbride, mother of John Kilbride. June 1964. Keith Bennett's mother died in 2012. She campaigned all her life for the chance to give her son a proper burial, but despite numerous searches Keith's remains still lie (2017) somewhere on Saddleworth.

(Above right). The poster of Keith which was circulated widely throughout the area.

Ann Downey, mother of Lesley Ann Downey stands near the searchers as they comb the moor for clues. She was not present when they found Lesley Ann's remains but identified clothing recovered from the grave as belonging to her daughter.

Lesley Ann Downey's uncle is restrained by police as Brady and Hindley leave Hyde Court after being remanded for Lesley Ann's murder. They were already being held for the murder of Edward Evans.

Mr Justice Fenton Atkinson described Brady and Hindley as "two sadistic killers of the upmost depravity". After the case, he wrote to the then Home Secretary, 'I did not make a recommendation in passing sentence because the only possible one would have been at that stage that neither should ever be set free again'. Further on he wrote, 'I hope Brady will not be released in any foreseeable future (assuming his fellow prisoners allow him to live) and that Hindley (apart from some dramatic conversion) will be kept in prison for a very long time'.

Some of the crowd gathered outside Chester Crown Court awaiting the arrival of Brady and Hindley for their trial before Mr Justice Fenton Atkinson. *Daily Mirror* crime reporter Brian Crowther covered the trial. He later recalled the scene in the courtroom when the tape of Lesley Ann Downey was played. "There was utter silence as we listened to the little girl pleading". He also said "Policemen walked out of court because they could not bear it anymore. No-one who heard that tape could ever escape from the memory".

Grandstand?

The Northern Counties Women's AAA Championships at Huyton in June 1960. Dorothy Hyman (4) winning the 100yds in 11.4secs from P Hall (Salford Harriers & Athletics Club) and C Carter (Liverpool Harriers & Athletics Club).

In our second image from the same meeting, Anne Oliver (94) wins the 880yds from S Newall (Sale Harriers) and A Laggett (Mitcham Athletics Club). Results of the competition were: Dorothy Hyman 100yds in 11.4secs and 220yds in 25.2secs. Joyce Grieveson won the 440yds in 60seconds dead whilst Anne Oliver won both the 880yds and the mile. Betty Moore won the 80metres hurdles and Dorothy Shirley the high jump. Audrey Spencer won the shot, Jean Heath the discus and Sally Scholes the javelin. The heptathlon was won by Barbara Brooks and J Gillyean the 5000metres track walk.

Distance runner Ron Hill gets a send-off from his colleagues at Courtaulds, Droylsden, as he heads off to the Tokyo Olympics where he finished eighteenth in the 10,000metres and nineteenth in the marathon. In 1963, Ron equalled the UK record for the 6mile (9.7km) at the British Amateur Athletics Association Championships. The following year he set his first world record when he clocked 1:15:22 for 25kilometres, knocking more than one minute off the legendary Emil Zatopek's time. Ron also won the 3-AAAs 10-mile (16km) every year between 1965-69, setting a new world record in 1968 of 46:44:0. In the 1968 Mexico Olympics, he finished 7th in the 10,000metres.

Prince Ade West of Nigeria practising to become a boxer at a gym in Atherton. August 1960.

Jim Cooper goes down for nine in the third round of his heavyweight fight against Chip Johnson at the Free Trade Hall, Manchester, on 9 November 1964. Jim, the twin brother of Commonwealth Heavyweight Champion Henry Cooper, had 31 professional fights in a career spanning 1954-1964. Of these, he won sixteen, lost fourteen and drew the other. Chip Johnson, from Naples, Florida, had 23 professional fights, winning ten, losing twelve and drawing one. The bout ended with Jim losing to Chip on a technical knock-out. It was to be Jim's last fight. On 20 April 1965, Chip took on Henry Cooper in a heavyweight bout at the Civic Hall, Wolverhampton. Our 'Enry won on points.

British Lightweight Champion Dave Charnley training in preparation for his title defence against Maurice Cullen at the King's Hall, Belle Vue. The fight took place on 20 May 1963, Charnley winning on points and in doing so winning his Lonsdale belt outright. A lack of suitable opponents then saw Charnley move up a division to welterweight and secure a bout against the world champion Emile Griffith. However, Charnley suffered such a beating that the referee stopped the bout in the eighth round. Charnley retired in 1964 as unbeaten British Lightweight Champion.

(Right) Brian London during his heavyweight bout with Henry Cooper at the King's Hall, Belle Vue, on 24 February 1964. To the winner would go the vacant EBU (European) Heavyweight, the BBB of C British Heavyweight, and the Commonwealth (British Empire) Heavyweight titles. London lost on points.

This wasn't the first time the pair had met in a title fight. The previous occasion had been at Earls Court in December 1959, when they fought for the BBB of C and Commonwealth titles. Then, too, London lost on points. They had also met in a heavyweight bout back in 1956, when London lost on a technical knock-out. Brian London had 58 professional bouts, winning 36 (25 by knock-outs), losing 21 and drawing one.

(Below) The referee signals the fight is over for 'The Manchester Midget' Tony Barlow in his bout against John McCluskey. The fight, for the vacant BBB of C British Flyweight Title, was held at the Free Trade Hall, Manchester, on 16 January 1967. Barlow, a brilliant amateur fighter, had 39 professional fights, winning 21, losing fourteen and drawing four. He retired in 1969 and later ran the Failsworth Boys Amateur Boxing Club.

(Left) A little over a month later, on 13 February, British Flyweight champion John McCluskey was in the ring at the King's Hall, Belle Vue, for a flyweight bout against Manolin Alvarez. McCluskey won on points. During a career spanning 1965-75, McCluskey had 38 professional bouts, winning 23 and losing fifteen.

(Below) Alan Rudkin celebrates regaining the BBB of C British Bantamweight Title with a win over Evan Armstrong at the King's Hall, Belle Vue, on 9 June 1969. Rudkin was a regular visitor to Manchester. His first bout in the city was against Brian Bissmire at the King's Hall on 20 May 1963. Rudkin's only bout at the Free Trade Hall took place on 9 March 1964, when he secured a win on points over Danny Lee. By the time Rudkin clashed with Baby John at the King's Hall on 30 November 1964, he had had eighteen fights, losing just one on a technical knockout. A year to the day later, Rudkin faced Fighting Harada at the Nippon Budokan, Tokyo, for a crack at both the WBC and WBA World Bantamweight titles.

Many of those who saw the fight would have made Rudkin a clear winner, but the judges thought differently and controversially awarded it to Harada. During 1966, Rudkin fought twice at the King's Hall - Edmundo Esparza (31 January) and Jose Bisbal (24 October) - winning both on points. In between he mounted an unsuccessful challenge for the Commonwealth (British Empire) and BBB of C British Bantamweight titles in a bout against Walter McGowan at the Empire Pool, Wembley, on 9 June. However, it was only a matter of time. On 13 May 1968, Rudkin challenged McGowan for his titles. The bout took place in a packed-to-the-rafters King's Hall and this time Rudkin secured win on points.

However, just ten months later, Rudkin was defending his Commonwealth title in a fight against Lionel Rose at the Kooyong Tennis Stadium, Melbourne, Australia. Rudkin lost. Had he won, he would have also taken the WBC and WBA World Bantamweight titles. His last bout at the King's Hall was the one pictured here. Rudkin had a career spanning 50 professional bouts, winning 42 and losing eight.

(Right) Fourth Test at Old Trafford on 1 August 1961. England had been set a second innings target of 256 runs in just 3hrs 56min playing time. At one point, it seemed as though England were going to win; they were 150-1. Then it all went pear-shaped as nine wickets tumbled in just two hours. Our image shows Alan Davidson taking Brian Statham's wicket. However, the real damage to England was caused by Ritchie Benaud who took 6 wickets for 70 runs. England were all out for 201; Australia winning by 54 runs with twenty minutes to spare.

(Bottom right). Fourth Test at Old Trafford, 29 July 1961. Bowler 'Fiery' Fred Trueman shouting at Subba Row as the unfortunate fielder drops Lawry. Australia's first innings ended at 190 runs all out from 63.4 overs with Statham getting 5 for 53. In reply, England's first innings ended at 367 all out from 163.4 overs. In their second innings, Australia amassed 432 runs all out from 171.4 overs leaving England to score 256.

(Below) Australian cricketers Graham McKenzie and Grahame Corling take shelter from the rain at Old Trafford. Fourth Test for the Ashes, July 1964.

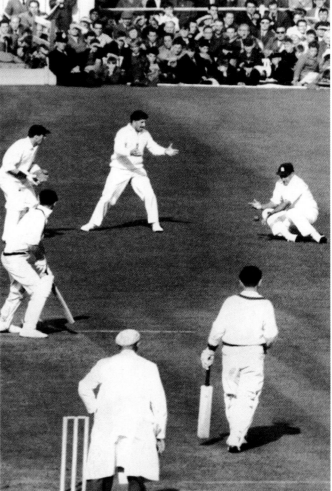

(Above) Flamboyant batsman and outstanding wicket keeper Farokh Engineer takes to the field on waste ground in Salford in a Test between England and Commonwealth players. It was for the Granada TV comedy series *Nice Time*.

(Below) Between 1953-60, wing-half Freddie Goodwin made 95 appearances for Manchester United scoring seven goals. In 1955-56, he also played as a fast-medium bowler in eleven matches for Lancashire County Cricket Club. In this match from July 1967, Bobby Charlton tries his hand at bowling during a Manchester v Timperley match, taking two wickets in three overs.

(Above) Goalmouth scramble as Blenheim Albion, a boys' team from Bolton, pile on the pressure against opponents Walkden Ladies during a charity match in December 1969. Ten-year-old Alan Hart, the youngest player on the field, is not shown any favours.

(Right) By the mid-1960s, ten pin bowling was all the rage. Introduced from the US in 1960, the sport caught on and the Rank Organisation took the opportunity to establish a major chain by converting cinemas into alleys.

Our image is of Mrs Joyce Atherton, of Long Lane, Chadderton, training at her home bowling alley in Oldham for the Daily Mirror ten pin bowling championship at Wembley Stadium Bowl on 17 July 1965. Mrs Atherton was in the finals of the women's singles handicap. After initial enthusiasm, interest in the sport rapidly diminished and many alleys closed.

(Above) Gerald Battrick on his way to defeating John Barrett 6-0, 6-4 in round three of the men's singles at the Northern Lawn Tennis Tournament, Didsbury, June 1969. He then lost the quarter finals to Thomas Gorman 6-3, 6-4, 14-12.

(Left) Australian Owen Davidson in action against Keith Wooldridge in the men's singles quarter finals at the Northern Lawn Tennis Tournament, Didsbury, June 1967. Davidson won 6-4, 6-2 and went on to win the final against Ray Ruffels 6-1, 6-8, 6-4.

Corrie star Jenny Moss, who played Lucille Hewitt, at the Northern Lawn Tennis Tournament at Didsbury, June 1965.

Former Wimbledon champion Fred Perry talking to the Junior British Champion Stanley Matthews Junior at a tournament at Didsbury on 7 June 1961. Stanley was the British Junior Champion 1960-62 and Wimbledon Boys Champion 1962.

Manchester racecourse, Castle Irwell, July 1960. In June 1952, Castle Irwell was where Queen Elizabeth II enjoyed her first winner as an owner since succeeding her father to the throne. The course was home to two major races: The Manchester November Handicap and the 1mile 3furlong Lancashire Oaks. When this picture was taken, the grandstand was so riddled with rot that it needed replacing. Its replacement was one of the first cantilevered reinforced concrete stands in the UK, but the cost was such that the course was plunged into financial difficulties. The shareholders decided to sell up.

(Right and below left and right) General view of the course in November 1963 before the last race meeting. The last winner of the Manchester November Handicap was *Best Song* ridden by Jimmy Lindley. Subsequently, the race was run at Doncaster where it became the November Handicap. The last winner of the Lancashire Oaks at Manchester was *Red Chorus*. The race was not run in 1964, but resumed in 1965 at Haydock Park. The Castle Irwell site was redeveloped by Salford University for halls of residence and playing fields.

(Right) From 1903 until his death in 1965, tipster Prince 'I gotta horse!' Monolulu was one of the most flamboyant characters in British racing. He claimed to be a prince of the Falasha tribe of Abyssinia though in reality he was Peter McKay from what is now part of the United States Virgin Islands. His first recorded appearance in feathers was at the 1903 Epsom Derby, though it was the 1920 Derby that made him. Punters who bought his tip that day would have backed the winner, the 100-6 outsider *Spion Kop*. Monolulu travelled to courses around the country including Manchester. Ever the showman, Monolulu appeared in three films. He died in hospital on 14 February 1965, not from his illness, but choking to death on a Black Magic strawberry cream chocolate.

(Left) United star Willie Morgan has a flutter on the nags at Haydock Park.

(Below left and right) A touch of Ascot comes to Manchester in June 1963 as staff from the Demmy betting shop, Oxford Road, turn up for work suitably attired for the occasion and punters place their bets for the Gold Cup. The favourite, Lady Sassoon's *Twilight Alley*, ridden by Lester Piggott and trained by Noel Murless, won by a length. William Hill, the world's biggest bookmakers, had its headquarters at Hill House, Manchester. Hills was founded in 1934 when only on-course betting was legal. Many people placed their off-course bets with a bookies runner, who would take the slips to the bookmaker and bring back the winnings. As a ten-year-old I ran my dad's bets for him on a Saturday morning as he was usually at work. There was nothing on the outside of the shop to show it was a bookmakers. All that changed with the Betting and Gaming Act 1960 which legalised bookmaking. However, on-street betting shops had to keep the door to the street closed as an open door could be interpreted as incitement to gamble.

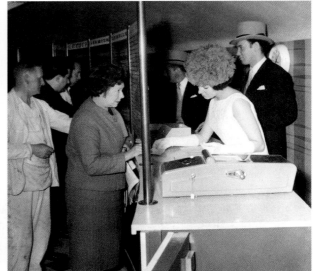

Leigh v Oldham, November 1969. Oldham stand-off Cliff Sayer is tackled by Leigh forward Welding and stand-off Eckersley. Cliff Sayer had two spells with Oldham, 1967-68 and 1971-72, making 45 appearances and scoring three tries. Of the two sides, Oldham had the better decade. They took the 1963-64 Division Two championship with 43 points (won 21, drew 1, lost 2), though Leigh finished second on 34 points (won 16, drew 2, lost 6). Rochdale Hornets were 8th on 17 points and Salford 12th on 16 points. In 1964 Oldham took Hull KR to three games to decide the semi-finals of the Challenge Cup and in 1966 they were beaten 16-13 by Wigan in the Lancashire Cup Final. The 1969-70 season was dire and heads rolled as Oldham finished next to bottom in the single 30-club division.

Leigh v Oldham, November 1969. Leigh prop Dave Chisnall is grounded by Oldham forwards Jim McCormack and Bob Irving. Jim McCormack made 165 appearances for Oldham, scoring 32 tries. Bob Irving made 296 appearances for the club, scoring 80 tries. While at Oldham, he was capped eleven times for Great Britain. On 16 December 1969, Leigh took on Wigan in the 1969 BBC2 Floodlit Trophy final which they won 6-11.

Leigh v Oldham, November 1969. Oldham centre Gary Beverley is tackled by Leigh second-row forward Geoff Lyon and stand-off Dave Eckersley. Geoff Lyon moved to Leigh from Wigan where he had made 328 appearances, scoring 73 tries. Geoff made 36 appearances for Leigh. Dave Eckersley played for Leigh until 1972 when he moved to St Helens, making 124 appearances, scoring 60 tries and five goals. In 1976, he moved to Widnes, making 167 appearances for them before packing his bags and trying his luck down under with the Cronulla-Sutherland Sharks, New South Wales.

Widnes take on Hull Kingston Rovers in the RL Challenge Cup Final at Wembley on 9 May 1964. Burwell of Hull KR goes down under a tackle from Frank Collier. Getting to the final had been something of a marathon for the Chemics. The First Round went to two replays before they could dispose of Leigh. In the Second Round, they beat Liverpool City at the first attempt, but the Third Round against Swinton also went to a replay. Even the semi-final against Castleford went to a replay, which Widnes won 15-3.

Widnes skipper Vince Karalius moves in to block a Hull KR attack. Born in Widnes, loose-forward Karalius, played 252 games for St Helens, scoring 42 tries. He joined Widnes in 1962, playing 128 games and scoring six tries.

(Above) Jim Measures tangles with the Hull KR defence giving Frank Collier time and room to sprint away and score Widnes's last try of the game. The final score was Widnes 13, Hull KR 5. It was the third time in their history that Widnes had won the Challenge Cup, having beaten St Helens 10-3 in 1930 and Keighley 18-5 in 1937. The club appeared in the 1950 final against Warrington but were thrashed 19-0. The 1964 Challenge Cup was their first trophy for eighteen years. It was also their only major success of the decade. Jim Measures played 133 games for Widnes, scoring 47 tries. In 1963, he was capped twice for Great Britain against Australia.

(Left) Skipper Vince Karalius is chaired off the pitch.

(Above) Widnes returned home to waiting crowds at the town hall, where a civic reception was held for the team.

(Right) Frank Collier holds the cup aloft to cheers from the fans. Frank Collier played 323 games for Wigan, scoring 26 tries and 27 goals. He played prop in Wigan's 27-3 win over Wakefield Trinity in the 1959-60 Championship final at Odsal Stadium, Bradford. He joined Widnes in 1964, playing 69 games and scoring 5 tries. He then joined Salford in 1966, playing 37 games for them. He was twice capped for Great Britain, in 1963 against Australia, and in 1964 against France.

Deprived of their usual cherry and white hooped jerseys, Wigan's 1960 Championship play-off squad for the final against Wakefield Trinity are pictured here in their training kit. Back row, left to right: Fred Griffiths, Geoff Lyon, Gerry Collingwood, Frank Collier, John Barton, Roy Evans and Keith Holden. Seated, left to right: Bill Sayer, Frank Halliwell, Syd Fenton, Eric Ashton, Billy Boston, Brian McTigue and Dave Bolton. Front: Terry Entwistle and Brian Scrivens. Wigan won 27-3.

In March 1962, six Wigan players were selected for the Great Britain squad against France. Left to right: Dave Bolton, Eric Ashton, Bill Sayer, Roy Evans, Billy Boston and Brian McTigue. Wigan signed Billy Boston for £150 in 1953 and in 1955 paid the same amount to sign Eric Ashton.

The 1963 RL Challenge Cup Final against Wakefield Trinity at Wembley. It was Wakefield's third appearance in the Challenge Cup in four years. Eric Ashton goes for the try but the referee blows for a penalty as Eric had already grounded the ball before crossing the line. Eric Ashton spent his entire senior playing career at Wigan during which he formed a formidable partnership with Billy Boston. Ashton played 497 games for the club, scoring 231 tries and 448 goals. Appointed player-coach in 1962, he was awarded an MBE in 1966 and retired from playing in 1969 though he remained as a coach.

Wigan centre Alan Davies grits his teeth as he approaches Trinity's right-wing Col Greenwood. Alan Davies joined Wigan from Oldham in 1961, playing 132 games and scoring 52 tries. He played in the side that won the 1961-62 Lancashire League and when the league was abolished in 1970 Wigan had won it no less than eighteen times. Davies left Wigan in 1965 playing a handful of games for Wakefield Trinity and then Salford. He was capped twice for England and twenty times for Great Britain.

Wigan lost against St Helens 12-6 and 25-10 against Wakefield Trinity in the 1961 and 1963 RL Challenge Cup Finals respectively. They finally brought the silverware back to Central Park in 1965 after beating Hunslet 20-16. Here, skipper Eric Ashton holds the Challenge Cup aloft as the team arrive at Wigan Town Hall. They were at Wembley the following year for the 1966 Challenge Cup: their opponents St Helens. However, it would not be a repeat of 1965 as Wigan were beaten 21-2.

Billy Boston and Frank Parr with the cup. At one point, ten-year-old fan Maurice Tait, of Lymefield Flats, Wigan, offered his dad's prized cup for fishing to Ray Ashby, but Ray declined the swop. Billy Boston spent fifteen years at Wigan during which he played 488 games, scored 478 tries and seven goals. Noted for his amazing turn of speed, Billy and Eric Ashton formed one of the finest partnerships in rugby league.

Ray Ashby is grabbed by enthusiastic fan 18-year-old Sadie Tinkin, of Marsh Green, Wigan. Ray played 124 games for Wigan, scoring 10 tries and one goal. He played full-back in Wigan's 20-16 win over Hunslet in the 1964-65 Challenge Cup final and in their 16-13 victory over Oldham in the 1966 Lancashire Cup.

Frank Parr and Ray Ashby show off the 1965 RL Challenge Cup to fans. Wigan's honours for the 1960s were: League Champions 1959-60. Challenge Cup Winners 1964-65. Lancashire Cup Winners 1966-67. Lancashire League Winners 1961-62 and 1969-70. BBC2 Floodlit Cup 1968-69.

Police contain demonstrators at the White City stadium on 26 November 1969. It was part of a nationwide protest movement against the tour of Britain and Ireland by the South African national rugby union side due to that country's policy of apartheid. It was also an attempt to force the cancellation of a tour by the South African cricket team scheduled for the summer of 1970. The game at White City went ahead, the Springboks beating North West Counties 12-9. On 6 December, the Springboks played a test match against Scotland at Murrayfield which they lost 3-6. The organiser of the Murrayfield anti-apartheid demonstration was future Prime Minister Gordon Brown.

Facebook Memories

Andy Spreckley – Dennis Law was a mate of my Grandad. When my Grandad had a massive stroke due to cancer he got him in at Maine Road for physio three times a week. A true gent.

John Edwards – Dennis Law and Ken Barnes were two very talented players – used to watch them both.

Alan Peters – I played against Peter Barnes when I was 15/16 and marked him out of the game. Ken Barnes came over to me afterwards and said what a good game I had. I didn't know who he was until my Dad told me! To be fair to Peter he was about two years younger than me at the time.

Funny Game Football

1 October 1960, Nat Lofthouse is challenged by Manchester United defender Bill Foulkes. The game ended 1-1. The 1959-60 season closed with Bolton Wanderers the top side in the area. They had finished in sixth place in the First Division with 48 points, three more than seventh placed Manchester United and eleven points clear of Manchester City.

A blistering shot from Wolves' outside-left Alan Hinton is enough to make Bolton's right-back Roy Hartle flinch. Hinton had one of the most powerful shots in the football league and could kick just as well with either foot. Such was his skill that, when taking a penalty, the goalkeeper had no idea which foot Hinton would kick the ball with until he did it. Luckily for Bolton, this shot was pushed for a corner by the Bolton keeper. This League Division One game from October 1963 ended 2-2.

20 February 1965, Bolton Wanderers entertain Liverpool in the Fifth Round of the FA Cup in front of 57,207 fans. Ian Callaghan scores the only goal of the game, causing a crowd surge behind the Wanderers' goal. The wooden railings collapsed and fans spilled out. Police and ambulance men rushed to the scene, but the ref played on.

(Above) Relegated at the end of the 1963-64 season, Bolton Wanderers hoped for a rapid return to top flight football. However, they finished the 1964-65 campaign in third place, six points adrift of runners-up Northampton Town. Our photograph was taken a couple of weeks before the start of the 1965-66 season. It would end with Manchester City promoted as Second Division Champions and Bolton in ninth position on 41points; ahead of Birmingham City and Crystal Palace on goal difference. In the FA cup, Bolton made it as far as the Fourth Round, where they held Preston North End 1-1 before losing the replay 2-3.

Despite playing in more than 600 professional football games, centre forward Bob Hatton had a somewhat transient career. He joined Bolton from Wolves in 1967, making 24 appearances and scoring two goals, before being transferred to Northampton Town in 1968. He also played for Carlisle United, Birmingham City, Blackpool, Luton Town, Sheffield United, Cardiff City and Dundalk.

1966 World Cup Tournament in the UK. Brazilian star Edson Arantes Do Nascimento – better known to most of us as Pele - takes a turn in goal during his team's training session at Bolton.

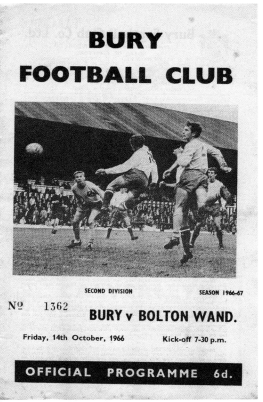

On 22 April 1961, Bury beat Hull 3-0 at Gigg Lane to clinch the Third Division title and promotion to the Second Division. The supporters' club presented the team with a cake in the shape of Gigg Lane at the championship celebration dinner.

Boxing Day 1962 and Bury were away to promotion contenders Sunderland. Our image shows Sunderland's prolific 29-yer-old goal scorer Brian Clough being stretchered off with medial and anterior cruciate ligament injuries following a collision with Shakers' keeper Chris Harker. The injury ended Clough's career as a player and launched him into the world of football management. After managing Hartlepools, Clough and his assistant Peter Taylor joined Second Division side Derby County in May 1967 and set about rebuilding the team. The plan worked and the Rams returned to the First Division at the end of the 1968-69 season.

11 January 1964, and Bury face an in-form Sunderland at Roker Park. The 4-1 win enabled Sunderland to keep up the pressure on Second Division leaders Leeds United who were just one point ahead. For Bury, the defeat left them in 20th position on 16 points, having played 24 games. Scunthorpe United, in 21st position, were also on 16 points but had a game in hand over Bury. Plymouth Argyle, propping up the Division on fifteen points, had played 27 games. At the end of the season, Sunderland were promoted as runners-up to Leeds United. Bury managed to scramble to safety, finishing in eighteenth position on 35 points.

Bury were at Ewood Park on 8 October 1966, where they faced Blackburn Rovers. The Shakers lost 2-1 and Blackburn Rovers climbed from tenth to seventh position in the Second Division. For Bury, the result left them in sixteenth place on nine points. At the end of the season, Blackburn finished fourth on 51 points: Bury were relegated after finishing bottom. Our image shows Blackburn's Bryan Douglas falling victim to Bury's hard-tackling centre back, Eddie Colquhoun. Colquhoun made 81 senior appearances for Bury before moving to West Bromwich Albion. It was the season Bury's tenure in the Second Division came to an end. Finishing bottom with just 28 points, they were relegated.

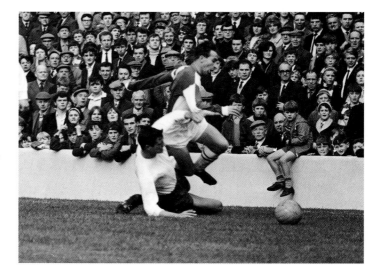

Manchester City

On 9 September 1959, City were at home to United and 58,300 fans watched as City won 3-0 with two goals from Joe Hayes and one from George Hannah. Our image is from the return fixture on 6 February 1960 and shows United keeper Harry Gregg clearing from George Hannah. The tie ended 0-0.

Bert Trautmann under pressure at White Hart Lane on 16 April 1960, as Spurs come close. Despite winning 0-1, City remained anchored in 18th place in the First Division with 33 points and four games left to play. Two days later, they lost 3-1 at Bolton Wanderers, though a win at Preston North End on 23 April lifted them to seventeenth place. On 30 April, a 0-1 win over Newcastle United at St James' Park took City to sixteenth position, though a 1-2 defeat at Maine Road by Burnley in their last game of the season saw them finish fifteenth on 37 points, ahead of Everton, Blackburn Rovers and Chelsea on goal difference.

Another image from White Hart Lane. Spurs finished the season in third place on 53 points, just two points behind Champions Burnley and one point behind runners-up Wolves. Spurs also got further than City in that season's FA Cup competition. Having defeated Newport County 0-4 in the Third Round, Spurs were drawn away to Crewe Alexandria in the Fourth. The Alex held Spurs 2-2 but the replay at White Hart Lane on 3 February 1960, ended 13-2. In the Fifth Round, Spurs drew a home tie against Blackburn Rovers and probably expected to win. They lost 1-3. City on the other hand went out in the Third Round, hammered 1-5 at Maine Road by in-form Southampton of the Third Division.

Denis Law and Ken Barnes pose for the camera in August 1960. Denis had been with City for just five months, having joined on a transfer from Huddersfield Town for the then British record fee of £55,000. On 28 January 1961, he scored all six (in just 48 minutes) of City's goals in their FA Cup Fourth Round tie against Luton Town, only for referee Kenny Tuck to abandon the game in the 69th minute. In July 1961, he was transferred to the Italian club Torino for £125,000. It was the first time a British player had commanded a six-figure fee. Wing-half Ken Barnes joined City in 1950 but did not become a first team regular until the 1954-55 season. Ken played a total of 283 games for City, scoring nineteen goals. In May 1961, he was appointed player-manager of Wrexham.

Following the abandonment of their FA Cup Fourth Round tie on 28 January 1961, City and Luton Town met four days later to replay the game. In the original tie, City had been 2-6 ahead. The replay was won by Luton 3-1 with Denis Law netting for City.

Division One action from 25 February 1961, as City take on Spurs at Maine Road. In front of 40,278 fans, City keeper Steve Fleet goes in Trautmann-style to whip the ball away from the feet of Spurs' forward Les Allen.

Liverpool full-back Ronnie Moran scores from the penalty spot on 22 August 1962. The match ended 2-2 with Neil Young scoring twice for City. This was City's second game of the season and the only one out of the first five in which they would earn a point. In the opening match, at Molineux, Wolves had systematically taken City apart to win 1-8. The third match of the season, a home tie against Villa, ended in a 0-2 defeat, and the trip to Anfield, on 29 August, ended 4-1 to Liverpool. The fifth game, against Spurs, ended in a 4-2 defeat. The writing was on the wall for City. They ended the season in 21st position on 31 points and were relegated.

Contemplating the future in relaxed mood with a pipe and a beer is sacked City manager George Poyser. As a player in the 1930s he had helped Brentford win the 1934-35 Second Division title, five points clear of Bolton Wanderers and eleven points clear of Manchester United. As a manager, his best season was with Notts County during 1954-55. They finished seventh in the Second Division and reached the Semi-finals of the FA Cup, disposing of First Division sides Sheffield Wednesday and Chelsea before going out 0-1 to Third Division (North) York City. In 1957, Poyser joined Manchester City as assistant to Les McDowell and replaced him as manager in July 1963 following City's relegation to the Second Division. The 1963-64 season ended with City in sixth place, though they enjoyed a run in the League Cup with victories over Carlisle United (2-0), Hull City (0-3), Leeds United (3-1) and Notts County (0-1), before going out 1-2 on aggregate to Stoke City in the semi-final. The following season, City finished in eleventh place and George had to go. He was replaced by Joe Mercer.

The end of the 1965-66 season saw City promoted as Second Division Champions. City's first game of the 1966-67 season was away at Southampton. Here Dave Connor beats Saints' half-back Ian White. The game ended 1-1. City ended the season in fifteenth position on 39 points. In the FA Cup competition, City made it to the Sixth Round where they were defeated 1-0 by Leeds United.

Instances of crowd violence at football matches have been recorded since the 1880s. When Blackburn Rovers played the Scottish side Queen's Park in the 1884 FA Cup Final at Kennington Oval, the *Pall Mall Gazette* described the Blackburn fans who had travelled to the game as "A northern horde of uncouth garb and strange oaths – like a tribe of Sudanese Arabs let loose". Allegedly, many of the Blackburn fans had been drinking heavily, were unruly, incomprehensible, and looking for trouble. In 1885 a game between Preston North End and Aston Villa ended with players of both teams being pelted with stones and physically attacked by 'roughs'. Groups of 'roughs' were bent on causing trouble – especially at local derby matches. The concept of fans following their teams to away games was something of a novelty, so it was not unknown for 'roughs' to attack the referee and the opposing team's players. Football hooliganism had arrived and remained a common occurrence throughout the last two decades of the nineteenth century.

By the 1930s, hooliganism was no longer a major problem but it re-emerged in the early 1960s with reports of fighting between rival fans. However, the violence tended to be confined to football grounds. By the late 1960s, hooliganism had become a serious problem. The 'roughs' were back in the form of organised gangs. At home games these gang members would congregate in the same part of the ground at every match and God help any away fans who happened to end up among them. The trouble also began spilling out of the grounds and into the surrounding streets both before and after matches. Games were now requiring intense levels of policing and the segregation of fans. Though called the English Disease, hooliganism was rife throughout much of Europe.

Our image was taken at the opening game of the 1967-68 season, when fighting between City and Liverpool supporters broke out during the match.

On 9 December 1967, third placed City were at home to fifth placed Tottenham Hotspur. Though the game was being televised on *Match of the Day*, nearly 36,000 fans battled through the snow and ice to Maine Road. Though the pitch itself was like a sheet of ice, City captain Tony Book had a cunning plan. He recalled that in his amateur football days with Peasedown St John, they would remove the top layer of leather from their boot studs to expose part of the nails that held the studs together. The exposed nails would give extra grip in icy conditions.

Referee Mr D W Smith inspected the pitch twice before declaring it fit to play on. Early on, the Spur's keeper Pat Jennings managed to deflect a shot from Alan Oakes. Despite the conditions, it was Spurs who opened the scoring with a goal from Jimmy Greaves in the sixth minute. Mike Doyle was unlucky not to get the equaliser when he fired a shot across the goalmouth that only just missed going in.

The bottom image shows the goal-mouth scramble involving Mike Summerbee, Francis Lee and Colin Bell that led to City's equaliser. The ball eventually landed at the feet of Colin Bell, who hammered it home. Mike Summerbee put City in the lead, and winger Tony Coleman made it 3-1 when he hit home a goal-post rebound off a shot from Francis Lee. Neil Young made it 4-1 to City and was unlucky not to score again when he hit the post.

After the match, Spurs manager Bill Nicholson said, "While we were slithering and sliding about, they played as if the conditions just didn't exist. They just ignored everything but their work, and under the circumstances they are certainly the best team we have met this season".

(Top) United and City clash at Old Trafford on 27 March 1968. Just four days earlier City had been beaten by Leeds United. Leeds were in top position with 45 points though only on goal difference from Manchester United. City were lying third on 43 points. Goals from Colin Bell, George Heslop and Francis Lee gave City the 1-3 victory.

(Middle) The battle for the 1968 First Division Championship went to the wire. Going into their final matches, City and United were level on 56 points, though City had the better goal average. Close behind on 53 points and with a game in hand was Liverpool. If City and United both lost and Liverpool won their remaining two games, the Merseysiders would take the Championship. City were away at St James's Park facing a Newcastle side that was probably still smarting from its previous week's 6-0 hammering by United at Old Trafford. Once again, Manchester United were at home; their opponents Sunderland. Liverpool were also at home against Nottingham Forest.

In front of 46,492 fans, Mike Summerbee got a touch to a ball from Mike Doyle to put City ahead in the thirteenth minute. Newcastle were soon level when a pass from Jackie Sinclair found Bryan Robson who placed the ball in the back of the net. Neil Young made it 2-1 to City. Young scored again but his goal was disallowed for off side. Newcastle came back again and pulled level with a goal from Jackie Sinclair. At half time, it was 2-2. After the break, Neil Young again put City ahead and in the 63rd minute Francis Lee made in 4-2 despite an appeal for off-side. With time running out, John McNamee pulled one back for Newcastle but City held on for a 4-3 win.

United had been favourites to win, as they were playing bottom-half Sunderland at Old Trafford, but against the odds the Wearsiders pulled off a 2-1 victory. It was City's first Championship since 1937. Liverpool had beaten Forest 6-1. They still had Stoke City on 15 May and, if they could win, they would jump over United and take the runner-up position. Stoke won 1-2. City were Champions with 58 points, United runners-up on 56 points, and Liverpool third on 55 points.

Our image shows Francis Lee scoring City's fourth goal.

(Bottom) George Heslop (left) and Colin Bell celebrate City becoming Champions. 11 May 1968.

In 1965 Joe Mercer signed 22-year-old winger Mike Summerbee from Swindon Town for £35,000. It was one of the bargains of the 1960s for Summerbee would join up with Colin Bell and Francis Lee to form what would become one of the most dynamic – and entertaining - strike forces in the First Division. During his career at City, Summerbee made a total of 452 appearances, scoring 68 goals and making many more. He received his first England cap on 24 February 1968 for a match against Scotland at Hampden Park.

(Above) Midfielder Alan Oakes holds the club record for the number of appearances, 564 in a professional career spanning sixteen years. He joined City as an amateur in 1958, turning professional the following year. A consistent player, he appeared in all games but one during City's Championship winning season of 1967-68. In 1976, he was appointed player-manager of Chester City, making 211 appearances for them. Our image dates from August 1969.

(Bottom left) The week before City played Leicester in the 1969 FA Cup Final, Tony Book was at the Café Royal to receive the Football Writers' Association Footballer of the Year award. It was awarded jointly with Dave Mackay of Derby County (left). Standing between them is England manager Sir Alf Ramsey. Book's footballing career was unusual in that much of his playing career was spent with non-league clubs Frome Town and Bath City. Book joined Plymouth Argyle in 1964, signing for City in 1966. The following year he was made captain, skippering the side to the 1968 League Championship, victory in the 1969 FA Cup Final and both the 1970 European Cup Winners Cup and League Cup. He made 244 senior appearances for City.

(Left) The strips to be worn by Leicester City and Manchester City at the 1969 FA Cup Final get their first public airing on a quiet street in Wilmslow. From left to right wearing the Leicester kit are: Eve Atkinson, Ann Earls and Georgia Thompson. Sporting the Manchester City strip are: Ann Williamson, Linda Ward and Phillis Andrews.

(Right) Manchester City players Alan Oakes, Mike Doyle, Colin Bell, Neil Young and Tony Coleman at Piccadilly where they boarded the train taking the team to London to play Leicester City in the 1969 FA Cup Final.

(Bottom left) Manchester City manager Joe Mercer waves to fans as the team's train pulls out of Piccadilly.

(Bottom right) Malcolm Allison, City's assistant manager, being interviewed by the press prior to the 1969 FA Cup Final kick off

'Can you see me mother?' City fans at Wembley for the 1969 FA Cup Final against Leicester City.

1969 FA Cup Final. City striker Neil Young heads for goal.

Neil Young heads for goal only to be robbed by Leicester City keeper Peter Shilton. It was City's first appearance in an FA Cup Final since 1956 and Leicester's third in ten years; the others being 1961 and 1963. On paper, City were expected to take relegation-bound Leicester apart but it turned out to be a close-run thing. The final whistle meant Leicester shared a unique double with City – Cup runners-up and relegated. City had done it in 1926.

(Right) Mike Summerbee in action.

(Below) Skipper and joint Footballer of the Year Tony Book raises the cup.

(Below right) Lap of honour.

Fans line the streets of Manchester as City make their way to the Town Hall with the FA Cup.

City were at the Baseball Ground on 18 October 1969. Joe Corrigan punches the ball clear from the head of Dave Mackay following a corner. City won 0-1.

European Cup Winners Cup First Round Second Leg against Bilbao at Maine Road, October 1969. Bilbao keeper Iribar gets his hands to the ball. City won 3-0.

European Cup Winners Cup Second Round Second Leg. City take on Belgian side Lierse SK at Maine Road. The game ended 5-0 to City and our image shows Colin Bell scoring his second goal. Further wins against Academica de Coimbra and Schalke put City into the final against Gornik Zabrze which was played in Vienna on 29 April 1970.

Manchester City take on Leeds United at Maine Road on 29 November 1969. Leeds keeper Gary Sprake manages to tip the ball away from Tommy Booth's head. Born in Middleton, Booth joined City in 1965 signing professional forms in 1967. He made his League debut in a match against Arsenal in October 1968.

City were at home to United on 3 December 1969, in the Football League Cup Semi-final First Leg, winning 2-1. The Second leg, played on 17 December, ended 2-2, earning City a place in the final against West Bromwich Albion.

Facebook Memories

John David Myles – Ken Barnes in his time was known as the best uncapped player in the country – the brains behind the Revie plan!

Jane Richardson – It was brilliant watching George Best play. A genius. And Bobby Charlton too.

Joan Terry – Wonderful picture of Sir Matt Busby and Joe Mercer in the paper the other day. Both true greats and gentlemen of the game.

Manchester United

Busby Babe and Munich survivor Albert Scanlon was not too happy in August 1960 having been dropped from the forthcoming derby game against City. The left winger said "I'm not happy about it. As a team, we haven't been playing well. I don't think I've been playing well either". After making 115 appearances for United, Albert was sold to Newcastle in November 1960, making 22 appearances for them.

The move did not work out and in 1962 Albert moved to Lincoln City, making 47 appearances for them before moving to Mansfield Town in 1963. Albert played 108 senior games for Mansfield, leaving in 1966 for non-league club Belper Town. After Munich, United's nickname 'the Busby Babes' no longer seemed appropriate. It had largely been manufactured by the media to describe United's youthful 1956-57 Championship side that went into Europe the following season. Though there was media talk of rebuilding 'the Babes,' Matt Busby preferred the Red Devils.

Between 1961 and 1964, inside right Phil Chisnall made 35 senior appearances for United, scoring eight goals. He was transferred to Liverpool for £25,000 and made his debut for them in a tie against Arsenal in what was BBC television's first Match of the Day. To date (2017) he remains the last player to be directly transferred between Anfield and Old Trafford. Chisnall left Anfield in 1967 having made only eight senior appearances. He moved to Southend United, where he made 142 appearances, scoring 28 goals.

(Right and middle) The winter of 1962-63 was one of the most severe for many years and affected all aspects of life including sport. Over a six-week period, more than 400 League and cup games were postponed or abandoned, the worse day being 9 February, when only seven of 64 scheduled English and Scottish League games were completed. On Boxing Day 1962, United beat Fulham 0-1 at Craven Cottage but they had to wait until 23 February 1963 to play a game all the way through to full time when they took on Blackpool. During the following April, United completed seven league games and beat Southampton in the FA Cup Semi-final to secure a place at Wembley. At the start of May, they still had seven league games to play as well as the FA Cup Final.

On 1 May, they met Sheffield Wednesday at Old Trafford and lost 1-3. Three days later they were at Turf Moor where they beat Burnley 0-1. Over the next sixteen days, they played against Arsenal (lost 2-3), Birmingham City (lost 1-2), Manchester City (1-1), Leyton Orient (won 3-1) and Nottingham Forest (lost 2-3). Our images are from the game against Burnley on 4 May. In the first one, Burnley centre half John Talbut, performs a perfect overhead kick to clear a United attack as teammate Brian Miller and United's Albert Quixall look on. Our second image shows Burnley keeper Adam Blacklaw kneeling to gather a cracker of a shot from Bobby Charlton as Denis Law closes ready to pounce.

(Bottom right) Because of the backlog, the season was extended and the FA Cup Final between Leicester City and United did not take place until 25 May 1963.

The final was to be broadcast live on BBC Television but there was a problem. The blue shirts of Leicester City and the red ones of United would be indistinguishable to viewers as the BBC transmitted in black and white, so the corporation asked if one side would change its strip. The teams tossed a coin and Leicester lost. There was no such problem for Pathe News as they filmed in colour.

The first fifteen minutes or so proved nerve-racking for United, as Leicester's Ken Keyworth, Mike Stringfellow and Dave Gibson all squandered chances. United eventually settled down and in the 30th minute Denis Law blasted the ball past two defenders and goalie Gordon Banks to open the scoring. The above image shows Gordon Banks diving as he tries to save Law's shot.

1963 FA Cup Final. This image, taken ten minutes after the previous one, shows Denis Law on the verge of scoring a second goal. Having beaten Gordon Banks, Law was unable to steer the ball into the net due to pressure from the Leicester defenders. David Herd put United 0-2 up in the 57th minute, when he deflected a parry from Gordon Banks into the back of the net. In the 80th minute, a superb diving header from Leicester City's Ken Keyworth made in 1-2. With five minutes to go, United were again piling on the pressure in the Leicester half. Johnny Giles fired a cross which Gordon Banks came off his line to intercept. Banks, usually a safe pair of hands, fumbled the ball and it fell to the feet of David Herd, who turned and fired it past two City defenders for United's third.

A legend in the making. George Best made his league debut against West Bromwich Albion on 14 September 1963. His next first team appearance came on 28 December, when he was picked to play in the home tie against Burnley. This image shows George (extreme left) celebrating his first league goal in the 5-1 win. Matt Busby decided to keep George in the team and by the end of the season he had made 26 appearances, scoring six goals.

The 1963-64 FA Cup competition was going well for United. In previous rounds, they had disposed of Southampton 3-2, Bristol Rovers 4-1 and Barnsley 4-0. In the Sixth Round, they were then drawn at home against Sunderland. The tie ended 3-3 and went to a replay, which ended 2-2. The second replay was held at Huddersfield on 9 March. Here, United's keeper Dave Gaskell punches the ball clear from Sunderland's George Herd during a rare attack by the Wearsiders. United won 5-1, with goals from Denis Law (3), Phil Chisnall and David Herd. United drew West Ham United in the Semi-finals, losing 1-3.

Midfielder Pat Crerand on the ball for United during a match against Fulham at Craven Cottage on 5 September 1964. Fulham won 2-1. Pat joined United from Celtic in 1963, going on to make 304 senior appearances, scoring ten goals. He retired from playing in 1971 but stayed on at Old Trafford as a coach and later as assistant manager to Tommy Docherty. In 1976 he was appointed manager of Northampton Town.

On 8 September 1964, United drew 3-3 away at Everton and just four days later were at home to Nottingham Forest. Here George Best and Forest's Joe Wilson go for the ball. The game ended in a 3-0 victory for United, thanks to goals by David Herd (2) and John Connelly. Connelly joined United from Burnley in 1964, making 113 appearances and scoring 35 goals. He was transferred to newly relegated Blackburn Rovers for £40,000 in time for the start of the 1966-67 season.

(Top right) It is 26 September 1964, and 53,058 fans are at Old Trafford to watch United play Tottenham Hotspur. Here, Spurs' midfielder Alan Mullery ends up in the back of the net following a futile attempt to stop Dennis Law scoring. The match ended 4-1 with Pat Crerand and Dennis Law scoring two apiece. Between 8 September and 5 December, United would enjoy a run of fifteen league games without defeat, including handing out a 7-0 hammering to Aston Villa.

(Middle) The 1964-65 FA Cup Semi-final against Leeds United at Hillsborough was a heated affair. Here Bobby Charlton intervenes to stop Pat Crerand sorting out Billy Bremner, whilst Denis Law is being pulled away from Jack Charlton by Bobby Collins. The match ended 0-0. The replay, at the City Ground, Nottingham, was won 0-1 by Leeds thanks to a goal from Billy Bremner.

(Bottom right) The 1966 FA Cup was United's last chance that season for a trophy. Despite some high scoring victories in the League, 0-5 away at Leicester City, 5-1, 6-2, and 6-1 home wins against Spurs, Northampton Town and Aston Villa respectively, fifteen draws and six defeats resulted in United finishing fourth. In the European Cup, a goal by Nobby Stiles in the Semi-final, second leg, was not enough to wipe out Partizan Belgrade's lead. This image is from the FA Cup Semi-final against Everton at Burnden Park, Bolton, 23 April 1966. Everton's keeper Gordon West makes a flying save from David Herd. A second half goal from Everton's Colin Harvey was enough to put the Merseysiders into the final.

After being dumped out of the League Cup 5-1 by Blackpool on 14 September 1966, and beaten in the FA Cup Fourth Round 1-2 at Old Trafford by Second Division Norwich City, United's fans might well have been wondering what the season would bring. It brought the First Division Championship. George Best turns on the magic at Upton Park on 6 May 1967 as United take the Hammers apart in front of 38,424 fans. After twenty minutes, Bobby Charlton, George Best, Bill Foulkes and Pat Crerand all had their names on the score sheet. The match ended 1-6 with Denis Law netting the other two. As soon as they heard the news that United's rivals for the title, Nottingham Forest and Tottenham Hotspur, could no longer overtake the Red Devils the fans celebrated with a pitch invasion.

United had already won the 1966-67 First Division Championship having taken West Ham United apart at the seams 1-6 on 6 May. However, they still had a game in hand - a home tie against Stoke City on 13 May. It was not the biggest Old Trafford gate of the season; that had been 62,727 for the match against Nottingham Forest on the 11 February. Nevertheless, 61,071 fans turned up to watch the 0-0 draw. Afterwards the players were joined on the pitch by manager Matt Busby and the Championship trophy.

The FA Charity Shield at Old Trafford on 12 August 1967 ended 3-3. Spurs keeper Pat Jennings stops John Aston as Joe Kinnear blocks Brian Kidd.

Alex Stepney (Big Al) joined United from Chelsea in 1966 for £55,000 which at the time was a world-record record transfer fee for a goalkeeper. Stepney made 539 appearances for United of which 433 were for the first team in domestic games. Big Al was noted for pulling off some superb saves and United fans know how important his close-range save from Eusebio was during the European Cup Final against Benfica.

On the other hand, Stepney was on the receiving end of one of the freakiest goals of the 1960s, when during the 1967 Charity Shield, Spurs' goalkeeper Pat Jennings put one past him. From his own 18yd box Jennings kicked the ball from his hands in a long lob up field which then bounced over Big Al and into the net. Then again there were occasions when Stepney was called upon to take penalties and he did score two goals.

George Best, Pat Crerand, Frank McLintock and John Radford jump for the high ball during the Division One tie between United and Arsenal at Old Trafford in October 1967. United won 1-0. This image came second in the sports category of the World Press Awards.

November 1967. Matt Busby receives the Freedom of Manchester from Lord Mayor Alderman Mrs Elizabeth Yarwood.

29 May 1968 and United are at Wembley for the European Cup Final against Benfica, a side that had already won the trophy twice. To reach the final, United had seen off Hibernian, Sarajevo, Gornik Zabrze and five-times winners Real Madrid. Benfica had beaten Glentoran, Saint Etienne, Vajas and Juventus.

Bobby Charlton opened the scoring in the 53rd minute with a rare header, though Benfica levelled in the 75th minute with a goal from Jamie Garcia. Benfica might well have won had it not been for Alex Stepney who saved in a one-on-one duel with the great Eusebio. The game went to extra time. Just three minutes in, George Best picked up a long ball from Alex Stepney, dribbled his way round the defence and put the ball past Henrique to make it 2-1. One minute later Brian Kidd made it 3-1 and a few minutes later Bobby Charlton scored his second.

United were the first English side to win the European Cup. Since its inception in 1956, Real Madrid had won it five times, Benfica twice, Inter Milan three times, AC Milan and Celtic once each.

United show off the latest addition to their trophy cabinet during an open-top ride through the streets of Manchester.

The scene in St Ann's Square, where an estimated 250,000 people had gathered to welcome back Manchester United following their victory in the 1968 European Cup Final.

United pose with the European Cup. Matt Busby received a knighthood.

(Right) At the end of the 1968-69 season, Sir Matt Busby stood down though he remained at Old Trafford as general manager. His place was taken by 31-year-old Wilf McGuiness. Under McGuiness, United finished the 1969-70 season in eighth position in the First Division and won the third-place play-off in the FA Cup. They also reached two semi-finals in the League Cup.

Denis Law beats Southampton's Tony Byrne to the ball during the match at Old Trafford on 16 August 1969. United lost 1-4.

(Bottom) Nottingham Forest's Terry Hennessey attempts a tackle on John Aston. The match, played at Old Trafford on 18 October 1969, ended 1-1.

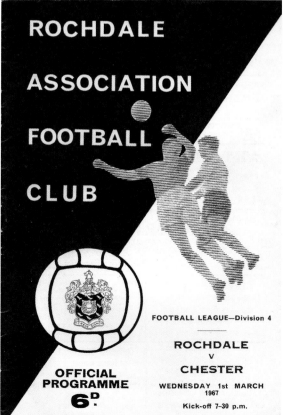

ROCHDALE

ASSOCIATION

FOOTBALL

CLUB

FOOTBALL LEAGUE—Division 4

ROCHDALE
v
CHESTER

WEDNESDAY 1st MARCH
1967

Kick-off 7-30 p.m.

OFFICIAL
PROGRAMME
6ᴰ.

Rochdale FC 1961-62 season. Back row left to right: Milburn, Hepton, Wragg, Burgin, Winton, Phoenix and Cairns. Front row left to right: Aspden, Thompson, Bimpson and Whitaker.

The season ended with Oldham, Rochdale and Stockport County occupying eleventh, twelfth and sixteenth positions respectively in the Fourth Division and whilst Manchester United had reached the Semi-finals of the FA Cup, lowly Rochdale had reached the final of the League Cup and would play Norwich City of the Second Division. This was a relatively new competition voted in at the annual meeting of the League in 1960 and created to give clubs in lower divisions the chance of winning a bit of silverware. The main difference between the FA Cup and League Cup finals was that the latter was to be played over two legs.

The First Leg, played at Rochdale on 26 April 1962, attracted just 11,123 fans, who watched as the tractor fanciers romped home 0-3. The Second Leg, played at Norwich on 1 May, attracted 19,708 fans and again Norwich were the victors winning 1-0. Some of the First Division sides had declined to take part in either the 1960-61 or 1961-62 competitions and a total attendance of 30,831 over a two-leg final did little to change their minds.

Rochdale remained in the Fourth Division for most of the decade, though finishing the 1968-69 season in third place on 56 points gave them promotion to the Third Division. Despite losing only two of their last 24 games, Rochdale still needed to take a point off Southend in the very last fixture of the season. Steve Melledew opened the scoring for Rochdale in the fifteenth minute and in the 67th Reg Jenkins made it 2-0. With ten minutes to go, Reg converted a Smith cross to make it 3-0.

Wigan Athletic FC

Throughout much of the 1960s, Wigan Athletic FC were members of the Cheshire League. They were the 1964-65 Cheshire League champions, with Harry Lyon their top scorer with 66 goals. During the 1966-67 season, the club won the Lancashire Floodlit Cup, the Liverpool Non-League Senior Cup, the Northern Floodlit League, and the Northern Floodlit League Cup. In 1968, they were founder members of the Northern Premier League.

During the 1960s, Wigan regularly made it through the qualifying rounds of the FA Cup to enter the draw for the First Round Proper, when Third and Fourth Division clubs entered the competition. The qualifying rounds for the 1962-63 FA Cup saw Wigan dish out a 5-0 thrashing to Milnthorpe Corinthians and an 8-1 hammering to Fleetwood, as well as winning 0-3 away at Netherfield and 2-0 at home to Ellesmere Port Town. Hopes of progressing beyond the First-Round Proper ended when they lost 2-1 at Gateshead. Their 1964-65 FA Cup campaign again ended in the First Round Proper when they were beaten 2-1 away by Stockport County.

In the First-Round Proper of the 1965-66 competition, Wigan were drawn away to Doncaster Rovers who they held to a 2-2 draw. Four days later Wigan won the replay 3-1. However, any thoughts of Wigan progressing 'Roy of the Rovers' style to the final were soon dashed when they were beaten 2-1 away at Chester in the next round. Interestingly, Doncaster Rovers went on to win promotion as Fourth Division Champions, though for them too the dream was short-lived as they were relegated at the end of the following season. Wigan were again in the First-Round Proper for the 1966-67 FA Cup. They held Tranmere Rovers 1-1 but lost the replay 0-1 at home.

After a short gap, Wigan made it to the First-Round Proper of the 1969-70 FA Cup. On 15 November 1969, they held Port Vale 1-1 at home. Three days later, the first replay ended 2-2, however, the second replay ended 1-0 in favour of Port Vale.

(Top right) With just eighteen minutes gone in the FA Cup First Round Proper replay against Doncaster Rovers at Springfield Park on 17 November 1965, Wigan Athletic centre forward Harry Lyon received an ankle injury and was stretchered off. Following treatment, Lyon limped back on and scored a hat trick. Here he is scoring his first.

(Middle) Harry Lyon piles on the pressure.

(Bottom right) Wigan Athletic celebrate their 3-1 victory over Doncaster Rovers.

Rock 'n' Pop, Rhythm 'n' Blues

Promoted by Larry Parnes, *The Rock 'n Trad Spectacular* – The New Noise of 1960 was a massive forty-five venue tour starring Billy Fury and Joe Brown. The show played the Manchester Free Trade Hall on 7 October, and returned to the city on 14 November for a week at the Manchester Hippodrome. The show was such a hit that additional venues were arranged and it ended with a one-week residency at the Newcastle Empire commencing 5 December. Among the support acts was a young pianist by the name of Georgie Fame – real name Clive Powell. Born in Leigh, Powell's undoubted talent was evident by the time he was sixteen. Following an audition, he was signed by Larry Parnes as a backing musician and changed his name. He was one of Parnes' musicians chosen by Billy Fury to form his personal backing group The Blue Flames. At the end of 1961 there was some sort of disagreement between Fury and The Blue Flames, resulting in them parting company. They became Georgie Fame and The Blue Flames and eventually obtained a residency at the Flamingo Club, where their debut album *Rhythm And Blues at the Flamingo Club* was recorded live in 1963. It failed to chart though their follow-up album Fame at Last reached number fifteen. During 1964, the group appeared five times on *Ready, Steady, Go*. They also had three number one singles before Fame went solo in 1966.

The Platters appeared at the Free Trade Hall, Manchester, on 16 January 1960. The Support included Cuddly Duddly, who in real life was Jamaican-born singer David Heslop. Cuddly Duddly was marketed as Britain's first black rock 'n' roller, releasing a cover of Chuck Berry's *Too Pooped To Pop*. Interestingly, Heslop appeared on *Ho Boy!* no less than 21 times – more than any other artist, though Cliff Richard got close with 20. The Platters were also supported by Carl Barriteau and His Band. On 17 January, The Platters appeared on Val Parnell's Sunday Night at the London Palladium. The Platters are, back row left to right: David Lynch and Paul Robi. Front row, left to right: Tony Williams, Zola Taylor and Herb Reed.

Voted the top British vocal act of 1958 by readers of the *New Musical Express*, The Mudlarks were a family act comprising Jeff, Mary and Fred Mudd. When Jeff Mudd was called up for national service, he was replaced by David Lane (David Burgess) a talented compere and entertainer from Collyhurst, Manchester. In November 1961, they headlined a short one-nighter tour along with the Temperance Seven. Also appearing were Bert Weedon, Joan Small, and Tommy Sanderson and The Sandmen. Our picture, dating from November 1961, shows Mary visiting Jeff (on the left) and Fred in Crumpsall Hospital, where they had been taken following a road accident.

Winning a talent contest eventually led Eden Kane to a recording contract with Decca and his first single, *Well I Ask You*, went to number one in August 1961. His next three singles all made it into the top ten but the fifth failed to chart. Kane parted company with Decca and signed up with Fontana. When this photograph of Kane was taken in Manchester, in September 1963, he was visiting local record stores promoting his single *Like I Love You*. Kane appeared at the Essoldo, Stockport, on 23 February 1963, on a bill that included Joe Brown, Susan Maughan, Shane Fenton and The Fentones, and Jess Conrad.

The one and only Eddie Cochran. Eddie was a highly talented singer-songwriter who could play piano, guitar, bass and drums, as well as pioneering the use of multitrack recording and overdubbing. His was a fusion of rock 'n' roll and rockabilly and his hits included *Summertime Blues, C'mon Everybody, Somethin' Else* and *Three Steps To Heaven*. 1959 proved to be a bad year for rock 'n' roll when Buddy Holly, Ritchie Valens and the Big Bopper were killed in a plane crash. 1960 would be no better when on 17 April, Eddie Cochran died of injuries sustained in a road accident on the A4 at Chippenham, Wiltshire, during his UK tour.

A young police cadet by the name of David Harman is said to have been amongst the first to arrive on the scene. A few years later he would be better known as Dave Dee of Dave Dee, Dozy, Beaky, Mitch and Titch. Another link with Eddie was a young boy named Marc Feld, who carried Cochran's guitar to his car after a gig. He would be better known to us as Marc Bolan.

The Beatles' third single *From Me to You* was top of the charts when they appeared at the Manchester Odeon on 30 May 1963. Written by Paul McCartney and John Lennon, *From Me to You* was released on 11 April, and was the group's first official number one. Their first single, *Love Me Do*, was released on 5 October 1962, and the following day the group were at Dawson's Record Shop, Widnes, signing copies in what would be the first of many such events. Despite receiving air time on Radio Luxembourg, *Love Me Do* only reached number 17 in the UK charts.

On 17 October, the Beatles were in Manchester to record their TV debut on Granada's *People and Places*. The boys returned to Manchester on 25 October to record for the BBC radio programme *Here We Go* at the Playhouse Theatre. On 7 November, they were back at Granada recording their second appearance on *People and Places*. The group's second single, *Please Please Me*, was released on 11 January 1963, and though many charts would list it as reaching number one, the all-important Record Retailers' Chart placed it at number two. Interestingly, though *From Me to You* failed to chart for the Beatles in the US, a cover by Del Shannon did. *From Me to You* was also the last song to be released with its writing credits as Paul McCartney and John Lennon, and the first of a run of eleven consecutive number one singles.

(Bottom left and right). It is 13 October 1964, and the Beatles are on stage at Wigan ABC. It was a similar scene the following evening when they performed at the ABC Cinema, Ardwick. Also on the bill were Mary Wells, Tommy Quickly, The Remo Four, Sounds Incorporated, Michael Haslam, and The Rustiks. Prior to appearing at Ardwick, the Beatles recorded an appearance for Granada TV's *Scene At 6.30*.

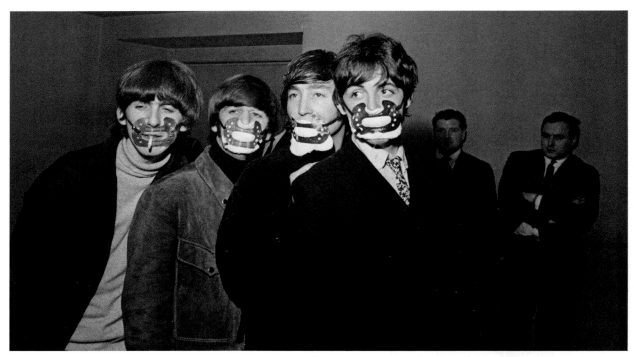

(Top and Bottom left) Two images from *The Beatles Show* at the ABC Cinema, Ardwick, on 7 December 1965. Promoted by Brian Epstein and Arthur Howes, the show coincided with the release of the Beatles' *Rubber Soul* LP. In one of the photographs, the boys, wearing smog masks, arrived at the ABC with just five minutes to spare before going on stage. Also appearing were the Moody Blues, the Marionettes, the Paramounts, Koobas, and Beryl Marsden with Steve Aldo. A seat in the front stalls would have set you back 15s.0d.

(Above) Beatles wallpaper produced by Wall Paper Manufacturers Ltd, Manchester. In September 2016, a single roll of this paper was on sale on E-bay for £279.99p.

In the early 1960s, some groups hardly ever moved about the stage. The same could never be said about Manchester's very own Freddie and The Dreamers as they were noted for their wacky routines. Just to prove it, here is 5ft 3ins tall Freddie Garrity bouncing around during a gig in April 1964. Between May 1963 and November 1964, they had four Top Ten hits, *If You Gotta Make a Fool of Somebody, I'm Telling You Now, You Were Made for Me*, and *I Understand. I'm Telling You Now*, which was co-written by Freddie and Mitch Murray, reached the top of the US charts in 1965. The group appeared in four movies including *Crazy World* which starred Joe Brown.

At 6.35pm on Wednesday, 1 January 1964, the BBC broadcast *Top of the Pops* live from Studio A at Dickenson Road, Rusholme. Performing live, but miming to their records, were: Dusty Springfield (*I Only Want to be with You*), The Rolling Stones (*I Wanna be your Man*), The Hollies (*Stay*), the Swinging Blue Jeans (*Hippy Hippy Shake*) and the Dave Clark Five (*Glad All Over*). On film were Cliff Richard and The Shadows (*Don't Talk to Him*) and Freddie and The Dreamers (*You Were Made for Me*). Pictured here are the Dave Clark Five, who knocked The Beatles' *I Want to Hold Your Hand* off the top of the charts.

Jamaican-born singer Millie Small rehearsing her bluebeat hit *My Boy Lollipop* for BBC's *Top of the Pops* at the Dickenson Road Studios, Rusholme. Millie's record was released in March 1964 and by the week ending 7 May it was at number two in the UK charts. Despite selling 600,000 copies, any hopes Millie had of dislodging *Don't Throw Your Love Away* by The Searchers from top position were dashed when fifth placed *Juliet* by The Four Pennies went to number one during the week ending 21 May. Millie was the first performer in British pop history to have a hit with a bluebeat record.

Dusty Springfield and Bobby Vee exchange autographs during the interval at the Odeon, Manchester, on 5 May 1964. They were on a 29-date tour along with The Searchers and Big Dee Irwin. On 9 May, they played the Bolton Odeon. Seats at Bolton cost 10/6d, 8/6d, 6/6d and 5/6d (53p, 43p, 33p and 28p).

Vee's break into the industry came following the deaths of Buddy Holly, Ritchie Valens and the Big Bopper in a plane crash on 3 February 1959 during their Winter Dance Party tour of the US. They had been due to perform at Moorhead, Minnesota, but the only top act left on the bill was Dion. Valens (aged 15) and band comprising boys from a school in Fargo volunteered to go on. They were given Holly's slot and were a hit. Valens was good enough to be signed by Minnesota-based Soma Records, releasing his first single *Suzie Baby* later that year. He followed this with a cover of Adam Faith's *What Do You Want?* Vee had a string of Top 10 UK and US hits including: *Rubber Ball, Take Good Care of My Baby* and *Than I Can Say*.

Dusty Springfield first came to prominence in the folk group the Springfields which she formed in 1960 with her brother Tom. She went solo in 1963, enjoying chart success with her single *I Only Want to Be with You*. During 1964 she had hits with *Wishin' and Hopin'* (also recorded by the Merseybeats) and *I Just Don't Know what to Do with Myself*.

Originally formed as a skiffle group by John McNally and Mike Pender, the Searchers' first single for Pye Records, *Sweets for My Sweet*, was a UK No.1 hit in 1963 with their follow-up release *Sugar and Spice* making it to No.2. The Searchers proved astute at covering US hits including *Needles and Pins* and Jackie de Shannon's *When You Walk in the Room*. Our image shows the Searchers line-up as many of us remember it. Left to right: John McNally, Chris Curtis, Tony Jackson and Mike Pender.

Another location used by Granada was the disused Wilbraham Road railway station, where the *Blues* and *Gospel Train* was filmed on 7 May 1964. During April and May 1964, the *Blues and Gospel Caravan* toured Europe and featured the talents of Muddy Waters, Sister Rosetta Tharpe, Little Willie Smith, Otis Spann and Ransom Knowling. Having arrived in a horse-drawn carriage, Sister Rosetta strolled along the rain-soaked platform, picked up her guitar and sang the aptly titled *Didn't It Rain*. The performers were on one platform, the audience on the other.

(Right) The legend around Manchester of how Wayne Fontana and the Mindbenders came into being goes something like this. Fontana and Bob Lang were members of a group named the Jets. The Jets secured an audition at the Oasis Club but only Fontana and Lang turned up as the group had split. They press-ganged drummer Ric Rothwell and guitarist Eric Stewart into taking part and thus Wayne Fontana and the Mindbenders were formed complete with a two-year recording contract from Fontana Records in their hot little hands. Success was not immediate but Fontana stuck by them and their fifth single, *Um, Um, Um, Um, Um,* reached number five in the UK charts. This was quickly followed by a top-ten selling EP and an album.

Their follow-up single, a superb rendition of Clint Ballard's *Game of Love* went to number two both in the UK and US. In October 1965, Fontana suddenly upped sticks and left in the middle of a concert, leaving Eric Stewart to pick up the vocals. The group continued as the Mindbenders and enjoyed chart success with *A Groovy Kind of Love* which went to number two and *Ashes to Ashes* which made it to number fourteen. Bob Lang quit in March 1968 and was replaced by Graham Gouldman. A few months later the Mindbenders broke up. Graham Gouldman and Eric Stewart went on to form 10cc.

(Middle) Manchester group Herman's Hermits pictured at the Kingsway Recording Studios in December 1965, where they were recording tracks for the movie *Hold On!* Directed by Arthur Lubin, the film stars the band as themselves on tour across the US. It was the Hermits' second outing on the silver screen. The previous year they had appeared as themselves in *When the Boys Meet the Girls*.

(Bottom right). 'The king of Rhythm and Blues', Chuck Berry and his backing for the tour, The Five Dimensions, tune up during rehearsals at the Manchester Odeon on 10 January 1965. Berry was accompanied on the 24-date tour by Long John Baldry and the Hoochie Coochie Men, The Graham Bond Organization, The Moody Blues, and Winston G. The Five Dimensions also played their own set.

(Top right). Keith Richard of the Rolling Stones signs autographs for a lucky few. The Stones had just recorded an appearance for *Scene at 6.30*. We are not sure of the date of this image but think it was taken in March 1965.

(Top left and middle) The fans get a little lively as the Rolling Stones perform at the Apollo Theatre, Manchester, on 28 September 1966. During the year, the group toured Australia, Europe and the United States. Also on the bill at Manchester were Ike and Tina Turner, the Yardbirds, Peter Jay and the New Jaywalkers, the Kings of Rhythm Orchestra, Jimmy Thomas, Bobby John, and Long John Baldry. UK singles hits for the Stones during 1966 were *19th Nervous Breakdown*, which reached number two, *Paint It Black*, which topped the charts during May and *Have You Seen Your Mother Baby, Standing In The Shadow?* which reached number five. On 13 April 1964, a Stones' gig at the Cubi Klub, Rochdale, was cancelled after trouble broke out among the 1500 fans attempting to get in. Matters were not helped by the fact that three of the Stones had been delayed due to a flat tyre.

(Bottom left) At least one girl fan made it onto the stage. She attempted to grab Mick Jagger but was quickly removed by security.

Manchester Free Trade Hall is where, on 17 May 1966, Bob Dylan experienced his now famous 'Judas' moment in what Andy Kershaw later described as the "the most famous heckle in rock 'n' roll history". The American folk singer/songwriter had already caused a stir at the 1965 Newport Folk Festival, Rhode Island. On the first day, he played his set using an acoustic guitar. On the second day, he played electric guitar and was met with boos and cat calls from a large section of the crowd. Many folk fans thought that by using an electric guitar Dylan was selling out on his folk roots. However, by the time Dylan arrived in the UK in May 1966, he had already had five electric hit records in the UK charts so to think he would not do an electric set was, with hindsight, naïve.

On 10 May 1966, Bob Dylan and his backing group, The Hawks, kicked-off an eleven-date tour of the UK with a gig at Colston Hall, Bristol. On 17 May they were at the Free Trade Hall. The first set was a virtuoso solo performance from Dylan who used an acoustic guitar. The second set was something else. Dylan swopped to electric guitar and with help from the Hawks ratcheted up the sound, belting out *Tell Me Momma*.

That Dylan had gone electric was bad enough for many folkies. That the lyrics were mushed as the sound bounced around the auditorium creating an echo just made matters worse. The audience responded with murmurings, slow hand-clapping and jeers. Then, in a moment of stunned silence, someone up in the circle shouted "Judas!" Dylan heard it and shouted back "I don't believe you. You're a liar!" He then turned to the band and said "play loud!" or "play f*****g loud!" which they did, erupting into a high-energy rendition of *Like a Rolling Stone*.

Dylan's troubles were not over. Folkie traditionalists and poor acoustics plagued the tour. A review of one of the gigs at the Albert Hall told of a "…thunderous quintet who made it virtually impossible to distinguish a single line of the lyrics."

So, who shouted "Judas!" Originally, a guy by the name of Keith Butler was credited with the act, but after Andy Kershaw's documentary *Ghosts of Electricity – Bob Dylan at Manchester Free Trade Hall* was aired on radio 1, college lecturer John Cordwell got in touch with Kershaw claiming that he was the one. Kershaw's analysis is that yes Keith Butler was there and had joined in the heckling and that it is possible that they both shouted "Judas!" but that it is John Cordwell's voice that the microphones picked up.

A bootleg recording of the Free Trade Hall concert circulated for years, though it was incorrectly labelled as being one of the Royal Albert Hall gigs.

Of the tour – which included gigs in the US and Australian as well as the UK - Hawks' guitarist Robbie Robertson said that the electric set was booed and jeered at just about every night but "They were wrong. We were right". In late 1967 the Hawks changed their name to The Band, releasing their highly-acclaimed album *Music from Big Pink* in early 1968. The track *The Weight* was used in the movie *Easy Rider*.

June 1967 and The Monkees arrived at London Airport to the screams of hundreds of female fans. The group had formed during 1966, specifically for a new NBC TV series that mixed pop music and comedy in a Beatles meets the Marx Brothers sort of way. American actor/musicians Michael Nesmith, Peter Tork and Micky Dolenz (already known to UK TV audiences for his role in *Circus Boy*) were teamed up with British actor/singer Davy Jones. Davy, who was born in Openshaw, Manchester, already had a successful acting career having played the Artful Dodger in the original West End and Broadway runs of *Oliver!*. The Monkees TV show was aired for the first time in the UK on New Year's Day 1967, instantly catapulting their new single *I'm A Believer* to the top of the charts. In 1967 The Monkees outsold both the Beatles and the Rolling Stones.

Former Manchester College of Art student and pioneering blues singer John Mayall takes a nap between appearances. In 1962, Macclesfield-born Mayall teamed up with trumpeter John Rowlands, alto saxophonist Jack Massarik, rhythm guitarist Ray Cummins and drummer Hughie Flint in the Blues Syndicate, playing in the jazz/blues style championed by Alexis Korner. They appeared regularly at the Twisted Wheel nightclub, Brazennose Street, Manchester, though during 1963 Korner persuaded them to try their luck in London. By late 1963 they were appearing under the name the Bluesbreakers and in 1964 released their first single *Crawling Up a Hill*.

The following year they backed the legendary John Lee Hooker. Among the musicians who played with the Bluesbreakers were ex-Yardbirds guitarist Eric Clapton (1965-66 then formed Cream with Jack Bruce and Ginger Baker), Jack Bruce (1965-66 then to Manfred Mann), Mick Taylor (1966-69 then to the Rolling Stones) and Peter Green (1966-67 then formed Fleetwood Mac). The Twisted Wheel was Manchester's premier venue for blues music and the club's Autumn Programme for 1965 included: The Spencer Davis Group; the St Louis Union (from Chorlton and 1965 Melody Maker National Beat Contest winners); The Mojos; Zoot Money's Big Roll Band; Georgie Fame and The Blue Flames and the John Mayall Bluesbreakers.

From 1955 until August 1958, when their family emigrated to Australia, brothers Barry, Robin and Maurice Gibb lived in Chorlton-cum-Medlock, where with a couple of friends they had formed a skiffle/rock 'n' roll group the Rattlesnakes. In Australia, the brothers continued to play music and in 1960 they landed the job of entertaining the crowds during the interval at the Redcliffe Speedway Track. Television appearances and gigs at resorts along the Queensland coast followed and the group changed its name from the BGs to the Bee Gees. In 1962 they were the support act for Chubby Checker and the following year they were signed by Leedon Records. Their single *Spicks and Specks* (released in 1966) was voted Best Single of the Year by Australia's top-selling music magazine.

However, the group decided to try their chances back in the UK arriving in early 1967. The brother's father, Hugh Gibb, sent demo tapes to Brian Epstein and the Bee Gees were signed to Robert Stigwood's Polydor Records. Their first UK single was a re-issue of *Spicks and Specks*. A canny piece of marketing saw the advance copies sent out to radio stations with only the title of the track printed on the label. Some of the station DJs thought the single was a new release by the Beatles resulting in the disc getting a lot of air time and securing the group a top twenty hit. On 17 October 1967, the Bee Gees' release *Massachusetts* went to number one and stayed there for three weeks.

On 2 April 1967, the Bee Gees made their first appearance in Manchester when they played at the Palace Theatre along with Fats Domino – on his first UK tour – and Gerry and The Pacemakers. Our image from early 1967 shows Barry, Maurice and Robin Gibb with band members Colin Peterson and Vince Melouney.

(Top left) It is March 1967 and The Hollies with stand-in drummer Tony Mansfield pose for the camera during a break in rehearsals for *Doddy's Music Box*. The Hollies' regular drummer, Bobby Elliot, had collapsed on stage with an inflamed appendix and Tony Mansfield stood in for him so the group could honour tour commitments. Mansfield (real name Anthony Bookbinder and older brother of Elkie Brooks) had been a founder member of The Dakotas. Brian Epstein persuaded the group to back singer Billy J Kramer and billed them as Billy J Kramer with The Dakotas. The group recorded in its own right, reaching No.18 in the UK charts in 1963 with the instrumental *The Cruel Sea*. Mansfield left The Dakotas in 1966. (Top right). The Hollies on *Top of the Pops*.

(Middle). Cilla Black relaxes between filming the Beatles spectacular at Granada Studios in November 1965. Cilla went from cloakroom girl at the Cavern Club to international singing star after being introduced to Brian Epstein by John Lennon. Epstein signed Cilla and she remained his only female client. In February 1964, her second single, *Anyone Who Had a Heart*, spent three weeks at the top of the charts and her third release, *You're My World* also went to number one. Cilla's third single, *It's For You*, was written by John Lennon and Paul McCartney, with Paul playing piano on the recording. On the silver screen, Cilla sang *Is it Love?* in the 1965 film *Ferry 'Cross the Mersey*, and in 1966 sang the signature song to the movie *Alfie*. In 1968 she had a major part in *Work Is a Four-Letter Word*.

(Left). How tickled he is. Ken Dodd and Sandie Shaw on the set of *Doddy's Music Box* at the ABC Television Studios, Didsbury, January 1967.

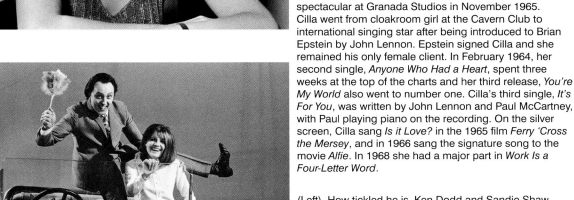

That's Entertainment

On 1 May 1962, singer Lonnie Donegan headlined the 'Spring Show' at the Palace Theatre, Manchester. Also on the bill were Jimmy Jewel and Ben Warriss - one of the great comedy double acts of the forties and fifties. Jewel and Warriss were first cousins and both had had solo careers prior to them getting together in the 1930s. Stars of stage, variety and radio, Jewel and Warriss also appeared in the 1946 Royal Variety Performance and went on to make regular appearances on TV. Around the time of the 'Spring Show', the pair were involved in a short-lived TV comedy series.

As can be seen on the poster on this page, Jamaican-born soul singer Jimmy James also featured in the show as a solo artist. In 1964, James teamed up with The Vagabonds to form Jimmy James and The Vagabonds and went on to record some of the earliest examples of Jamaican ska music to be recorded in the UK. From 1965 onwards, Jimmy James and The Vagabonds became a popular support band, featuring in tours headlined by the likes of The Who, Rolling Stones, Sonny and Cher and Jimi Hendrix. They disbanded in 1970.

Our image shows Lonnie rehearsing with The Debutantes.

(Above) Jimmy Jewel, Ben Warriss, Lonnie Donegan and Christine Carroll rehearse a sketch based on the *Daily Mirror* cartoon character Andy Capp.

Singer Marion Montgomery and Michael Segal (complete with Chicago typewriter) as they take a stroll in Manchester. They were two of the stars appearing in Cole Porter's *Anything Goes* at the Palace Theatre. Marion played Reno Sweeney, a night club queen, and Michael played second-rate gangster and public enemy 13, Moonface Martin.

Written by Leslie Bricusse and Anthony Newley, the musical *The Roar of the Greasepaint, The Smell of the of the Crowd* opened at the Theatre Royal, Nottingham, in August 1964, for an eight-week provincial run in anticipation that it would go to the West End. It starred Norman Wisdom, Willoughby Goddard, Sally Smith, Dilys Watling and Cy Grant. The plotline explored the maintenance of the status quo between the upper and lower classes of 1960s Britain. Among the show's songs were *A Wonderful Day Like Today* and *Who Can I Turn To?* Norman Wisdom is pictured with co-star Sally Smith and at the Palace Theatre, Manchester, during the show's final week on tour.

In 1963 Bolton-based playwright Bill Naughton had a West End hit with his comedy-drama *Alfie* which charts the womanizing antics of cockney chauffeur Alfie Elkins. This photograph was taken at the Mermaid Theatre on 17 July 1963. Alfie was played by John Neville. Also in the cast was a young actress by the name of Glenda Jackson (standing, second from right). Bill Naughton wrote the screenplay when *Alfie* was made into a movie starring Michael Caine. Cilla Black sang the Burt Bacharach/Hal David theme tune for the UK release, Cher for its release in the US. Bill Naughton was born in Ballyhaunis, County Mayo, in 1910, his family moving to Bolton in 1914. Bill's other 1963 play, *All in Good Time*, was a Broadway hit and in 1966 it too was turned into the movie titled *The Family Way*.

Don't look now. Shoppers scurry past the Town Hall steps, Bolton, as a couple of medieval knights fight it out. The knights were being filmed by the Octagon theatre.

The Octagon theatre at Bolton was opened by Princess Margaret on 27 November 1967. Its first production was *Annie and Fannie* by local playwright Bill Naughton. Our image is from December 1969, when for some reason the Octagon had need of an elephant.

(Top left). Shani Wallis, who played Miranda, with the one and only Tommy Cooper (left) and Alfred Marks, in the pantomime *Old King Cole* at the Palace Theatre, Manchester, 18 December 1962. (Top right). Panto time at the Palace Theatre, Manchester, in December 1967. Des O'Connor, the butt of many a Morecambe and Wise joke, is playing Buttons to Pippa Steel's Cinderella. No prizes for naming the panto.

The Victoria Theatre, Salford, was going through a rocky period in 1963 and was hanging on by a thread as a venue for live entertainment. The Manchester Evening News postbag received letters from readers who liked the friendly atmosphere of the Vic. As one reader put it, the Vic was "very different from the snotty attitude of the Opera House, impersonal atmosphere of the Palace, or clinical atmosphere of the Library Theatre."

(Top left) The Opera House, Quay Street, Manchester, was the January 1967 venue for The Bachelors All Star Comedy Show. Also on the bill was impressionist Mike Yarwood.

(Top right) *Corrie* star Pat Phoenix discusses her forthcoming role as Catherine in Tennessee William's *Suddenly Last Summer* with director Carl Paulsen at Oldham Rep's Coliseum theatre, Fairbottom Street.

When this photograph was taken in early 1969, Collyhurst-born comedian Les Dawson had just landed his biggest job – a six-week series of half-hour shows on Yorkshire TV. Les had worked the Northern club circuit - Manchester alone had more clubs than London and Birmingham put together – but it proved hard going and he was on the brink of giving up when, in 1967, he landed a slot on the ITV talent show *Opportunity Knocks*. Bookings on various TV shows followed but the Yorkshire TV series *Sez Lez* made him a household name. A talented pianist, Les entertained us by knowing just when to hit the wrong notes at the right time. His mother-in-law jokes were legend as was his gurning – the ability to pull grotesque faces. *Sez Lez* proved so popular that it ran for eleven series and 68 shows.

Archie Street in Salford's dockland was the location setting for the Granada TV soap *Coronation Street* and featured in the opening credits. In July 1969, the *Manchester Evening News* broke the news that the street known to millions of viewers around the world would soon be no more as the area was scheduled for demolition. St Clement's Church would be the only building to escape the bulldozers. United player Eddie Colman was born in Archie Street.

Pamela Craig (Jackie Marsh) and William Roache (Ken Barlow) on location in Bury in January 1966. Pamela's character was a reporter on a local newspaper; the story line being that whilst Ken's wife Valerie (played by Anne Reid) was struggling at home with nine-month-old twins, Ken was getting up close and personal with Jackie. The affair and a planned dirty weekend away was wrecked when the pair were spotted kissing by Elsie Tanner (played by Pat Phoenix).

The Rovers Return set. On the left is Eileen Derbyshire (Emily Nugent) and propping up the bar next to her is Graham Haberfield (Jerry Booth). Also in the picture is Jean Alexander (Hilda Ogden). The part of Jerry Booth was Graham Haberfield's first professional acting role which he secured in 1962 just after graduating from the Bristol Old Vic Drama School.

Bobby the *Corrie* cat with his handler on set in April 1968. In the *Corrie* story line, Bobby and his owner Minnie Caldwell (played by Margot Bryant) arrived on the street in 1962, when they moved into No.5 following Esther Hayes' departure. In 1968 Bobby disappeared and Minnie eventually took in a stray which she called Sunny Jim. As Minnie tended to get a little confused she renamed the cat Bobby. Bobby's claim to fame came in 1973 when he ate Albert Tatlock's pet homing pigeon Gilbert.

Sex and the Sixties arrives in *Corrie*. The story line in May 1968 is that Dennis Tanner (Philip Lowrie) and Jenny Sutton (Mitzi Rogers) are planning to marry and move to Bristol. Elsie tanner will not let them share a bed so Jenny is lodging with Minnie Caldwell. Elsie "It's my fault, love, I never taught him the facts of life". Jenny "That's all right, love, I did!".

The cast of *Corrie* on set in May 1968. Violet Carson (Ena Sharples) had just returned to the soap following a three-month cruise and promotional tour to Australia. Whilst in Australia she attended the 10th Annual TV Week Logie Awards in Melbourne and presented awards to some of the main winners. Violet is holding a TV Week magazine award. It is thought to have been presented to her as a memento of the occasion.

There would have been at least one TV Week award going spare after the ceremony, as that year the magazine failed to pick anyone for Best Female TV Actress category. The idea for Ena Sharples to wear a hairnet came from Violet herself. She had a fine head of hair and dreaded it falling victim to the machinations of Granada TV's make up department.

The master of suspense, film director Alfred Hitchcock, pays a visit to *Coronation Street's* Rovers Return set in studio 2 at Granada, June 1964. Amongst the movies he had already brought to the silver screen were: *The Man Who Knew Too Much* (1956), *Vertigo* (1958), *North by Northwest* (1959) and *Psycho* (1960). And still fresh in many a cinema-goer's mind, Hitchcock's 1963 offering *The Birds*.

Lucille Soong who played Jasmine Chong.

Miss Wendy performs her balancing act with a pigeon perched on the end of s sword. 41st International Circus

The Salvador Troupe and their sphere of activity! 41st International Circus.

(Left) The annual Christmas circus at Belle Vue was often described as the finest show in the northwest. Acts were signed from around the world to ensure audiences had a great time. These two images are of the Schlingloff Troupe during rehearsals for the 41st International Circus which ran from 19 December 1969 to 7 February 1970. Among the other acts were: Willi Mullens Caucasian Cavalry and Ponies; Robert Bros' Gigantic Elephants, and Strongman Samson with Delilah.

(Middle) Robert Bros' Berkshire Pigs at the 41st International Circus. Bought as piglets for £10 each, these highly intelligent animals were the only performing pigs in the UK and valued by Robert Bros at £400 each.

(Bottom left). The 41st International Circus also featured Harry Belli's Horse-Riding Tiger: to say nothing of the dog! Harry ran a small circus in the Netherlands. The Tiger was called *Byla*, his horse *Bulle* and the dog was *Jimmy*.

(Bottom Right) Carol McManus (aged four) and her sister Grace (aged two) with their father at Belle Vue. December 1969.